When Doctors Join Unions

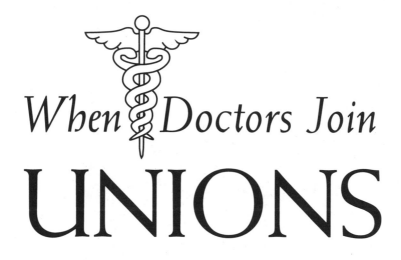

When Doctors Join

UNIONS

GRACE BUDRYS

ILR Press An Imprint of
CORNELL UNIVERSITY PRESS
Ithaca and London

First published 1997 by Cornell University Press.

Printed in the United States of America

Library of Congress Cataloging-in-Publication Data

Budrys, Grace, 1943–
    When doctors join unions / Grace Budrys.
        p.   cm.
    Includes bibliographical references and index.
    ISBN 0-8014-3277-4 (cloth : alk. paper).—ISBN 0-8014-8354-9
    (pbk. : alk. paper)
    1. Trade-unions—Physicians—United States.   2. Collective
    bargaining—Physicians—United States.   I. Title.
    R728.3.B83   1997
    610.69'52—dc20   96-32596

For M. B. and S. B.

whose views of doctors' work shaped the

questions I address here

Contents

Preface   ix

1   Introduction   1
2   The Eruption of the Physicians' Union Movement   8
3   Physicians' Strikes in the United States and Elsewhere   18
4   Professionalism: Construction of the Concept   32
5   The End of the Golden Age   39
6   The Union's Formative Years   48
7   The Changing Environment in the 1980s   59
8   The Deprofessionalization of Medicine?   64
9   The Mature Organization   73
10   Why a Union and Not a Professional Association?   87
11   From Cottage Industry to the Modern Era: The
Industrialization Model   97
12   Postindustrial Work: A New Class of Workers   106
13   Is It Legal for Doctors to Form Unions?   113
14   What Does the UAPD Do for Its Members?   127
15   A Physician's Union: Harbinger or Anomaly?   138
16   Other Unions and Their Future   145

Bibliography   157
Index   173

Preface

"Doctors were pushed off the pedestal. It was no accident." In the estimation of Dr. Sanford Marcus, founder of the largest doctors' union in the country, the pedestal-rocking began in the 1960s in reaction to the growing volume of patients' complaints: "They never listen!" "They're only interested in the money!" "They all drive Mercedeses!" "They treat us like we're stupid!" He maintains that the media reinforced the complaints, which encouraged political leaders to pass laws restricting physicians' privileges and corporate executives to implement the spirit of those laws by imposing bureaucratic controls. In the process, doctors lost the high standing they had enjoyed for so many years. Whatever society expected doctors to do in response to what they saw as strong, continuous, and unfair criticism, a physicians' union movement did not play a part in any of the scenarios.

If doctors' unions are a response to doctor-bashing, doctors have even more reason to unionize now than they did twenty years ago. The growing number of stories in the medical press documenting physicians' efforts to establish unions and unionlike organizations confirms the fact that a new wave of physician unionism is gaining momentum.

My interest in physicians' unions began with the first wave of organizing about twenty years ago. In 1977, I received a National Institute of Mental Health (NIMH) grant to study the union being established in the Chicago area, the Illinois Physicians Union. It was there that I discovered the existence of the Union of American Physicians and Dentists (UAPD), the subject of this book. I have followed its development in the medical and, occasionally, general press since that time.

A year of research leave from my University in 1992 permitted me to study the UAPD more closely. My phone call to Gary Robinson, the executive director, in April 1992 resulted in my being invited to the union headquarters in Oakland, California, to meet with him and Dr. Robert Weinmann, the current president of the UAPD. I found that Dr. Sanford Marcus, whose comments I had been following for many years, had retired from practice and from the presidency of the union. He invited me to meet with him at his home. In an interview that lasted several hours, he recounted the origins of the union, in a way that was as colorful as I had expected it to be from reading his comments in print. He made all his files in the union office available to me, and the next day, Gary Robinson and Dr. Weinmann gave me permission to carry out this study.

I returned to Oakland two months later to take up Gary Robinson's and Dr. Weinmann's offer to spend as much time as I liked interviewing staff and reading files. I spent a week there, collecting a large array of documents to ship home. I interviewed staff members, including the office manager who was the first person hired by Dr. Marcus over twenty years ago. I also met with union organizers, who interact with salaried physicians, and with staff members in the practice management department, which is primarily involved with physicians in private practice. I had more extended meetings with Dr. Weinmann and many conversations with Gary Robinson to clarify various points. I am grateful to everyone associated with the Union of American Physicians and Dentists and to persons associated with other labor organizations, their legal representatives, and others who have given generously of their time.

Over the years colleagues offered useful comments in response to related short papers and early drafts of this manuscript. I am indebted to all of them. I particularly thank Susan Sanders and Roberta Garner. Arthur Shostak and Lois Gray, who reviewed the manuscript on behalf of Cornell University Press, gave me many useful suggestions and provided a great deal of encouragement. I am especially grateful to Frances Benson for shepherding the manuscript from the time I submitted it to ILR Press to its, and her, new home at Cornell University Press. The two editors who worked on the manuscript, Kay Scheuer and Jane Slaughter, did more than correct my syntax and spelling. They raised challenging questions about statements that were not as self-evident as I had thought, and helped to clarify what I said in addition to how I said it. Finally, I wish to acknowledge the contribution of my husband, Dan Lortie. His support, understanding, and willingness to discuss the many and varied dimensions of this topic cannot be overstated. It was, however, his endless patience in telling me to "write what you mean" that made the book a reality.

GRACE BUDRYS

Chicago

When Doctors Join Unions

❧ 1 ❧

Introduction

This book documents the origins and development of the Union
of American Physicians and Dentists (UAPD). The story begins in 1972, the year the UAPD came into existence, and follows
its maturation over the next twenty years. The union was established
in the San Francisco Bay area by Dr. Sanford Marcus, who continued
as its president for eighteen years. Dr. Robert Weinmann, who succeeded Dr. Marcus, was elected president in 1990.

The history of the Union of American Physicians and Dentists is
intriguing. It unfolds to reveal a charismatic leader, critical early strategic decisions, and continuing opposition from hostile organizations in the union's environment. The heart of the story is how the
UAPD managed not only to survive, but to grow and develop over
two decades. It succeeded in avoiding the fate that befalls the vast
majority of groups that are born out of frustration but persist only so
long as the aggregate energy of a core of angry people provides
momentum. The UAPD attracted its initial following by capitalizing
on the mounting frustration doctors were experiencing during the
early 1970s. It would not have survived this long, however, if it offered nothing more than the opportunity to vent frustration. The
UAPD has been able to provide something more important.

The book presents a factual account of the practical problems
doctors must confront as they are swept along in the wake of rapid
change in the health sector. It documents the UAPD's attempts to
create problem-solving mechanisms for members. Beyond that, the
UAPD case points to broader trends, inviting further analysis and
interpretation.

Why does the emergence of this relatively small and atypical
union merit attention? Several alternative approaches for analyzing

the facts this case presents suggest themselves. Each raises a different set of questions.

One obvious framework for looking at this case is the health services approach, which encompasses the perspectives of those involved in hands-on health care delivery, policy makers, and other observers of the system. Use of this perspective is timely, because it responds to widespread concern about the turmoil in the health care delivery system. According to one set of experts, "American health care is in a state of hyper-turbulence characterized by accumulated waves of change in payment systems, delivery systems, technology, professional relations, and societal expectations" (Shortell, Gillies and Devers, 1995:131). Given the concerns central to this approach (which largely revolve around making organizations more efficient), the most noteworthy aspect of the UAPD story may be to discover what doctors are capable of achieving when they get serious about resolving work frustrations that are the by-products of such efficiency drives.

To the extent that health sector consultants are right in saying that "California is where health care trends originate" (Larkin, 1995:11), the UAPD may offer a preview of what the future holds for the rest of the country. Several facts, largely related to the reliance on competition currently favored by policy makers, point in this direction. There is an especially large concentration, possibly an over-supply, of doctors in California, particularly in the San Francisco Bay area (Mitka, 1992). According to the founder of the UAPD: "One of every 183 residents of San Francisco, has an M.D. degree, . . . about triple the national average" (Colburn, 1985:8). The well-established, not-for-profit managed care system located in that state is now being forced to compete with new, more aggressive for-profit managed care organizations (Robinson, 1991; Mitka, 1993). Some cities in California now have the highest concentration of persons receiving their health care through managed care organizations (Mitka, 1995). State legislation has given extensive privileges to allied health workers, a factor that certainly increases competition and, doctors say, increases their malpractice risk (Pickney, 1993). It is possible that consumers become more dissatisfied in response to their doctors' expressions of dissatisfaction, and this patient unhappiness is behind the attempt to vote in a single-payer plan that would eliminate competition (Somerville, 1994). The readiness to reduce taxes by cutting health care services to the poor is an indicator of the public's anger and frustration (Kirn, 1992).

An alternative framework for considering UAPD is the industrial relations perspective. Observers of the labor movement in this country have been concerned with the movement's fate for some years. Victor Gotbaum, who established the Samuel Gompers Leadership Award Program at the City University of New York, assesses the current situation: "Organized labor in the United States has entered a new era of economic constraints and political uncertainties unrivaled in its history. . . . These shifts and changes call for fresh ideas, new definitions and new models and paradigms" (1993:foreword).

Exploring the emergence of a doctors' union when union membership overall is clearly declining leads to two opposing assessments: one, this doctors' union is a fluke that may be interesting but holds limited significance for the union movement overall; or, two, the workers' organizations that evolved during the industrial era are being replaced by structures better suited to representing workers during the postindustrial era. As might be expected, I favor the second interpretation and support it in this book. In fact, I am suggesting that the UAPD may very well provide the model Gotbaum calls for.

Examining the case through the lens of organizational and occupational analysis offers a third, entirely different, perspective. Until recently the trends toward increased size and centralization have not greatly affected organizations that employ (or enter into contracts with) professionals and other highly educated workers. In this case, we see high-status professionals discovering the advantages that a union offers for bettering the conditions that govern their work. Unlike professional associations, which depend on their ability to persuade the public, government bodies, and other organizations, unions are able to address the problems of individual members far more directly, at the work site.

From this perspective, we can direct our attention to the processes through which occupational groups create their own identities and construct organizational structures to promote them. As the institutional environment in which they work changes, doctors are being pressed to identify their professional priorities and select the avenues they will use in pursuing them. Doctors are only beginning to discover that "managed care," the successor to the more limited health maintenance organization (HMO) designed to manage patients, is increasingly concerned with managing doctors.

The fact that 60 percent of the UAPD membership is in private practice reflects the level of concern among this category of California doctors, who, (compared to their colleagues in other states) are under an especially high degree of pressure to enter into managed care agreements. The other 40 percent of UAPD members are in salaried positions, working primarily for state and local government agencies and institutions.

Doctors across the country who believe that the realm in which they work is being poorly or unfairly managed are moving in directions that would have been considered radical only a few years ago. They are joining together into large practice groups to achieve increased bargaining leverage (Meyer, 1993a). My guess is that the formation of large practice groups will be the first step in a process through which doctors will learn to bargain collectively. Given that the medical profession has served as a model of occupational success, I am convinced that the advantages doctors achieve by organizing collectively are worthy of attention.

Finally, using a cross-national comparative perspective to assess the operations of this doctors' union provides a valuable corrective to the provincialism that prevails in the United States. In looking at work and workers in other countries we find, first, that union membership has not been declining in other industrialized countries to nearly the same extent as it has in the United States (Lipset, 1987). Second, we find that doctors are unionized in most other industrialized countries, where they apparently see less conflict between their professional identities and their union activities. Explaining why this is so requires an examination of the meanings Americans attach to unionism—its objectives, benefits, and drawbacks. Recognizing that unionism carries a certain negative connotation, which is apparently not present in other countries, suggests that we need to look more carefully at the cultural values and social expectations surrounding work and work organizations in this country.

These three perspectives are not entirely discrete; they overlap. Accordingly, I use an eclectic analytical approach, borrowing concepts and ideas from the various disciplines and bodies of literature the perspectives represent. This approach is also a response to the fact that the UAPD is an unfamiliar entity. The more common form of academic discourse involves innovative interpretations of familiar phenomena. This book proceeds from the opposite direction, introducing a new and different kind of organization, which, I believe, is better understood by being considered from several perspectives.

I present the UAPD's development chronologically against the background of changes taking place in its social and institutional environment. This is in recognition of the impact of external forces in shaping the union's identity, which evolved as the leadership made strategic choices to respond to those forces. First, I outline the emergence of the UAPD within the context of the social turmoil that characterized the latter half of the 1960s and early 1970s. I attempt to answer the basic question—why do *doctors* need a union? Since there are no survey data to indicate how the doctors who joined unions during those early years would have responded, I focus on the UAPD's answer to this question, an answer that undergoes considerable revision over time.

I then consider the most commonly raised objections to physicians' unions. One is that the ultimate weapon used by organized labor, the strike, makes physicians' unions unthinkable. I outline the circumstances that led to some of the most notable physicians' strikes and other forms of "job action" in this and other countries. I also consider the larger social context in which doctors bargain collectively in other countries.

Another charge against doctors' that they are unprofessional, and in an effort to lay the basis for making an informed judgment here, I examine the meanings attributed to professionalism over time, discussing the circumstances that precipitated shifts in the social definition of professionalism.

In exploring the UAPD's origins, we see that it came into existence at about the same time that approximately twenty-five other physicians' unions were being established. However, within a few years, the union movement lost its steam and the other unions faded away. New unions continued to appear, but few have persisted. This leads to the second question I propose to address in this book—what accounts for the fact that the UAPD was able to survive, indeed flourish, while other physicians' unions failed? I take up this question by focusing on the obstacles the UAPD confronted and overcame. I document the UAPD's changing activities as it adjusted to the shift in social and institutional realities from the 1970s to the 1980s. It is during this period that the medical profession began to move out of what some have defined as a "cottage industry" stage into a more advanced stage of production. The corporation executives who entered the health care sector during the 1980s brought with them a new, market-oriented perspective. They argued that medicine would benefit by being rationalized. They proceeded to reorganize health care delivery arrangements, bringing services under the control of larger, more centrally organized firms, differentiating the "products" they were offering, and providing a greater choice of services in response to consumer demand. I review the historical record of industrialization, when manufacturing changed from a cottage industry to a more modern form of production. This exercise permits me to compare the differences between the health sector, and the medical profession in particular, and other occupations and organizations that underwent industrialization to see what might be special to medicine.

I then return to medicine's professionalism to explore how its meaning is changing in adaptation to society's shift from an industrial to a postindustrial era. I take up, once again, the notion that there is an unresolvable conflict between professionalism and unionism. In looking at the UAPD during the 1980s, we find the union not only adjusting but becoming a mature organization. In this context I examine the differences between professional associations and unions and consider the legal restrictions on doctors' efforts to organize collectively.

The third basic question this book addresses is why would physicians choose to turn to a *union*? I consider the issue of what a physicians' union provides that doctors cannot obtain as readily elsewhere, particularly the innovative services such a union can offer its members. As this portion of the discussion makes clear, the UAPD uses a traditional union model to organize some of its functions but does not restrict itself to that model.

The discussion directly related to the growth of the UAPD ends with Chapter 15. The final chapter takes up the broader implications of this case. It is not only doctors who can learn from the UAPD's experience. Other occupational groups may also benefit, as they create new organizations and revise existing ones to address their respective needs. I also note some of the innovations being introduced by unions in other sectors. Those who think of unions as best suited to meet the needs of factory workers will be surprised to find, first, that nonindustrial unions are expanding, and, second, that they are experimenting with creative new approaches to address their members' needs, approaches substantially different from those traditionally employed by industrial unions.

❡ 2 ❡

The Eruption of the
Physicians' Union
Movement

I n reflecting on the origins of the Union of American Physicians and Dentists, Dr. Sanford Marcus remembers the turning point— the incident that turned him into a union activist.

> I can recall the event that radicalized me, if you will. It was a quarterly staff dinner at the hospital. The administrator got up and announced that the hospital was in the process of establishing an HMO. So I asked the administrator who was going to provide the medical services in this HMO. He said "You will, of course." So I asked if he didn't think he should have included the physicians in making the decision to found the HMO before he and the hospital board of directors decided to go ahead. His answer was that we would be included in the discussions, but that just had not happened yet. My reaction was—how can they do this to us? We're doctors![1]

This incident occurred early in 1972. Dr. Marcus responded by going home and composing a three-page letter addressed to all the physicians in the San Francisco Bay area. He was angry, and wanted other physicians to join him in resisting the treatment he felt they were all enduring without appropriate protest. He appealed to his colleagues' sense of injured pride.

[1] The quotes attributed to Dr. Marcus that do not include a specific citation are from interviews conducted in June 1992.

Let's tell it like it is—as a group we study more years, work longer hours, bear more crushing responsibilities, perform greater amounts of free service to our hospitals, teaching institutions, and communities, wade through more burdensome paperwork, are more constantly upgrading our skills, and generally give more of our inner selves to the betterment of society than any other group. We must now proclaim our right to demand appropriate payment for all of this! . . . [I]t is time we abandoned the canard that unselfish humanitarianism provides our only motivation. We have an unequaled record here, but in a society bent on grinding down the medical profession even our humanitarianism is minimized and ridiculed.

He took the letter to a local copying service and had 5,000 copies run off; he and his wife stuffed and addressed the envelopes at his dining room table. The letters indicated that a $25 fee was required to join the physicians' union that Dr. Marcus was proposing. He received 500 favorable responses, 250 of them including the $25. This permitted him to call an organizing meeting, and the group elected officers, wrote a charter document, and incorporated in the state of California. The Union of American Physicians and Dentists was established on April 18, 1972. The Preamble to its organizing charter reads:

We physicians and dentists, in order to provide optimum medical care for people; to insure quality facilities for the provisions of medical care; to enable doctors to give of themselves, unhindered by extraneous forces, for the welfare of their patients; to insure reasonable compensation for doctors commensurate with their training, skill and the responsibility they bear for the life and health of their fellow beings; do establish this Union.

When Dr. Marcus reflects on the factors that made him angry enough to devote himself to organizing physicians into a union, he admits to a mix of feelings. He told me that he was outraged at the way doctors were being treated. He did not like being "pushed off the pedestal." This reaction led him to the further admission that he and other doctors may have become too comfortable on that pedestal. This complicated set of reactions becomes clearer when he recalls his father's experience as a doctor, which he relates with considerable feeling. Although his father practiced during the Depression and did not make much money, he enjoyed the love and admiration of everyone in his community—people knew who he was and thought highly of him. Money is not the issue, Dr. Marcus says. What is most important is being able to do what is best for your patients and to have the patients know it and appreciate it.

But doctors can no longer do what they believe is best for their patients. In the years since Dr. Marcus entered practice, the environment in which doctors work has changed dramatically. To illustrate this, he points to the role of the hospital administrator. With a mischievous twinkle, he recalls what administrators were expected to do when he first began practicing: "All you expected of the person was that he would agree to wear a clean suit, stay sober, and come to work every day. His primary responsibility was to deal with the salesmen who came to the hospital." To show how things have changed, he says, shaking his head, when he first began organizing the union a hospital administrator told him: "One day you will all be working for us." Although this state of affairs is not yet completely true, the idea is not nearly as farfetched as it would have been even a few years ago.

In fact, Dr. Marcus says, doctors are now taking orders from all kinds of people who have no medical training. They must get pretreatment approval from an insurance company's clerical employee, located in some other city, possibly in another part of the country. Health care decisions are made by third parties, and doctors no longer have personal responsibility for their patients. That, according to Marcus, is the essence of the trouble. When you take away responsibility, you deny the person's ability to take pride in his work. There are different kinds of currency for doing high quality work: It's the physician's right to be the "best doctor he can be." Without that, medicine becomes menial work. He made the same point in his 1972 organizing letter: "There are three commodities for which we labor—money, the power to determine our own destinies, and intangibles such as honor or the satisfaction of healing."

Other Voices: The Physicians' Union Movement

Dr. Marcus and his colleagues in the San Francisco Bay area were not alone in their anger and frustration. Nor were they alone in choosing to form unions. Doctors all over the country were reacting similarly. A survey of 320 physicians carried out by the journal *Medical Economics* in 1972 found that 61 percent thought doctors should form a union; 11 percent were undecided; and only one in four was definitely against the idea (Bumke, 1987:82).

In another assessment, researchers found 16,000 doctors belonging to 26 unions or union-like organizations during the early 1970s (Bognanno, Dworkin, and Fashoyin, 1975). The medical press was filled with stories about physicians across the country organizing unions. The following examples indicate both the widespread nature of the phenomenon and the varied reasons physicians expressed for their new-found interest in unionization.

One of the most aggressive unions to emerge during this period was the Nevada Physicians Union. Organized in 1972, it was already well enough established by the following year to take action in response to what the members perceived to be a new and unacceptable demand by hospital administrators. The physicians were angered when the administrators of some Las Vegas hospitals began requiring them to put in one afternoon a week doing peer review of charts, to fulfill Medicare regulations. The union organized a "white-in" at Valley Hospital, which was certainly a "job action" but not exactly a strike. The doctors invited every patient who came to the emergency room to take a bed. They provided complete care both for those who chose to leave and for those who took beds; they simply neglected to fill out any of the necessary paperwork. The administration quickly succumbed, in a day and a half, agreeing to the union's terms. The union demanded a $50 per hour fee for doing chart reviews. The job action achieved the desired effect without depriving patients of medical care.

When the same situation arose in another hospital a year later, the union organized a similar job action. The administration of Sunrise, a 497-bed hospital owned by American Medicorp, Inc., offered no resistance, agreeing to sign the contract exactly as the union drew it up. The contract was similar to the one signed a year earlier with

Valley Hospital, but it contained one additional provision: no aspect of utilization review would be contracted out without prior approval from the union. This clause was necessary, according to union president Dr. John Holmes, because recently passed Medicare-Medicaid amendments would have permitted a nurse "to enter judgment as to the professional quality of care." The judgment would be reviewed by a physician "who could be buried in the bowels" of the Department of Health Education and Welfare in Washington ("Union Contract Binds . . . ," 1973). The Nevada Physicians Union's victory attracted wide attention from physicians and other interested parties across the country.

The circumstances that caused Dr. George Lagorio, the organizer of the Illinois Physicians Union, to become an activist are strikingly similar to those described by Dr. Marcus and others in the union movement across the country.[2] Dr. Lagorio recalls that the medical staff in his hospital deliberated a contract offer from a prepaid care organization and decided to reject it. The administrator of the hospital signed the agreement anyway. When Dr. Lagorio refused to sign the necessary forms, the administrator threatened to discipline him in front of his colleagues and to reduce his privileges. The medical staff executive council chose not to become involved in the situation. Dr. Lagorio told the administrator that he would sue if his privileges were reduced. The escalation of the terms of battle made him realize, he says, that no one was willing to support him in his stand against the hospital. It became obvious that collective action was the only means that would get the attention of the administration. He began organizing his colleagues in the spring of 1973.

The Illinois Physicians Union was chartered on June 5, 1973, in affiliation with the AFL-CIO. In one of the pieces of recruitment literature he authored, Dr. Lagorio explained why he thought a physicians' union was needed:

> Professional freedom is rapidly disappearing. Dignity, prestige and respect which are the symbols of medical professionalism have been eroded by insurance carriers and governmental

---

[2] The quotes attributed to Dr. Lagorio and other members of the Illinois Physicians Union are from a research project I carried out in 1977–78.

agencies desiring to gain control of medical practice, as well as the biased anti-physician diatribe of the press.

The physician has been made the "Whipping Boy" for the high cost of medical care in the United States. Unionism, under the protection granted pursuant to the Labor Laws of the United States, is a legal and acceptable American solution to the present-day American problem. In the final analysis, the physician who has joined organized labor has merely joined with his patient who is already a part of that movement, so as to achieve the ultimate goal of good medical care.

In San Antonio, Dr. Kenneth Burton, the general practitioner who launched the American Physicians Union of Texas, borrowed the "remember the Alamo" battle cry as his campaign theme in organizing the American Physicians Union. Burton said the response was "beyond belief." More than half of Bexor County's physicians signed up. This convinced him that he had a solid base from which to move ahead, "to cover all Texas and then the whole country" (Ferber, 1972:61). He presented a succinct argument for physician unionization:

> Why is it that doctors, among all the trades and professions, are alone in losing so much say over what they do and how they should be paid and are so close to surrendering their freedom? The answer is simple: Other elements in our society are strongly organized, while physicians haven't been willing to act collectively. (Burton, 1972:103, 108)

Dr. Burton went on to outline the factors, both internal and external to the profession, that stood in the way of broader physician unionization. One of the most important was doctors' individualism. He observed that physicians had not protested when restrictions on freedom of action in clinical matters were imposed on them "by the Government and other patient third parties" (Ferber, 1972:57). Now they were confronted with restrictions on economic matters, and again doing very little in response. In his view, the American Medical Association should have done more to support physicians in these matters, but clearly was not prepared to do so. An alternative to the

AMA that would unite doctors was essential, because the AMA was not accurately representing doctors' attitudes. Dr. Burton asked his colleagues to recall: "When did the AMA last take a vote to get its members' views on matters of urgent national interest?" (1972:108).

The second factor on which Dr. Burton focused was doctors' earnings. He blamed the press for spotlighting doctors' incomes. According to his calculations, physicians were earning about $11 an hour, less than many tradesmen. Apparently contradicting himself, he went on to argue, "Even if doctors as a profession are among the nation's highest earners, why should this single them out for blame? No one . . . heaps scorn on movie stars or pro football players because their incomes are in six figures. What's more, high earners like professional athletes and entertainers have unions to protect their interests, and no one seems to find anything objectionable about that" (Burton, 1972:109).

Finally, Burton discussed the services doctors provide: "The fact that physicians alone are guardians of the public's health is repeatedly cited as a reason for our not taking strong collective action against those who would weaken and eventually destroy our prerogatives. . . . [O]ur interests . . . coincide with the interests of our patients. It follows that if our working conditions deteriorate and the quality of our lives suffers, the patient care we provide will become less satisfactory" (Burton, 1972:109). Civic employees charged with safeguarding our lives, namely police and firemen, he noted, were unionized.

A statement by an internist from California is indicative of the depth of feeling that physicians were prepared to register in print:

> Forming a union is the only possible way that American doctors can save themselves from economic and professional slavery. Even more important, it's the only way that we'll be able to preserve and improve the quality of medical care. Every physician in my state has seen at first-hand how medical care deteriorates when a government agency imposes "practice by budget." . . . Only a strong national medical union that will stand up and fight can save us. (Burton, 1972:110–111)

Echoing the same sentiment, Dr. Harold Yount, president of the Florida-based American Physicians Guild, stated that the Guild's aim was to "act in any area of medical economics where the freedoms and rights of members are impinged upon" (Burton, 1972:112).

In an article discussing why he decided to join a union, New York physician Philip Alper makes it clear that he and others in widely scattered regions of the country were actively following the union movement. He joined a physicians' union because there was simply no other place to turn. In his view, no other organizations were powerful enough to stand up to the forces that were overtaking medical practice.

> Manipulation of huge sums of government money to favor one or another carrier, hospital, university, or health-delivery system has created severe strains. Add to this the role of politics and legal liability, and we see such things as hospital boards of directors who seize professional control of hospitals and dictate by-laws to medical staffs on a take-it-or-leave-it basis, as in Illinois; or universities that are embarking vigorously into the delivery of primary care at costs substantially above the going rate in the community, as in California. (Alper, 1974:28)

Opposing Voices

It is impossible to know what the majority of doctors were thinking privately about physician unionization during the early 1970s. A few essays did appear in the medical press opposed to physicians' unions—which does not, of course, mean that a small number of physicians were opposed. Some may have thought that the union movement had no relevance for them. Most were probably opposed. The majority were undoubtedly satisfied to watch from the sidelines.

A few individuals were, however, willing to take a strong stand in opposition. Dr. Michael Halberstam, for example, argued that though "unionization would give us some temporary bargaining power, we'd pay for it in loss of prestige, influence, and, quickly enough, in loss of income" (1973:75). "Medicine is *not* just another way to earn a living. First off, it's a profession, with all the characteristics that sociologists have deemed characteristics of the professions as opposed to mere occupations" (1973:76). He was especially opposed to physicians' relying on the strike to achieve their objectives:

"The main force of unionization is the threat to withhold services—
the strike—and a strike is the antithesis of everything the practice of
medicine is about" (1973:77–78).

The strike was a sensitive issue. Physicians who favored unions
were careful to stress that they were interested in helping patients
get better care and had no intention of withdrawing their services.
According to Dr. Stanley Peterson, president of the American Federation of Physicians and Dentists, which served for a time as the
umbrella organization unifying physicians' unions across the country, physicians had no intention of adopting Big Labor's pressure
tactics. The physicians' unions affiliated with the Federation were
not advocating striking, picketing, or creating procedures that would
restrict members' rights. "We'll deserve to be regarded as goons only
if we behave like goons, and that will never happen" (Ferber, 1973).

Most observers of medicine appear to have concluded that
strikes were unethical (Daniels, 1978). Others argued that this was
precisely why physicians' unions were necessary: without access to
the strike weapon, doctors needed organization to press their demands in other ways. In editing a volume on strikes in the health
care sector, Samuel Wolfe noted that he had made the same observation in the late 1960s. "We pointed out that in the next generation
the great majority of physicians will find themselves in bureaucratic
organizations. Such physicians ought to have the right to negotiate.
Increasingly, their goals will be more like those of other trade unionists" (Wolfe, 1975:6).

Dr. Burton of the American Physicians Union of Texas asserted
that strike actions would always be "unpalatable to doctors." However, he cast some doubt on his commitment to this position by
offering the added assurance that "even if we're forced to rely on that
ultimate weapon, we'd never go so far as to deny care to those who
really needed it" (Burton, 1972:108–110).

The Survival of Physicians' Unions

To the best of my knowledge, none of the 26 unions that
emerged during the early 1970s managed to survive except the
UAPD. Only one other physicians' union, which was established
even earlier, has persisted—the Doctors' Council. According to

Barry Liebowitz, who organized the Council in 1959 and continues to serve as its president, it employs a traditional union model and is proud to be a path breaker in recruiting high–status professional workers (Shostak, 1991:75). The union recruits physicians employed by both private and public hospitals and by health care organizations in New York City (Liebowitz, 1986). It has maintained a steady membership of approximately 3,000 doctors since it was established.

In the absence of more complete documentation, it is impossible to determine why the other unions failed to survive. One can reasonably conclude that they found it difficult to overcome the two most common objections voiced by opponents, that unionization is inconsistent with medical professionalism and that the ultimate bargaining tool unions rely upon, the strike, is unacceptable. It is hard to say to what extent the AMA's vigorous opposition to physician unions contributed to their demise. The AMA did not need to work very hard to convince doctors that unionization is inappropriate for such a high–status occupation as that of physicians. Not only doctors but the majority of Americans indicate that they see the role of unions from a similar perspective. (I address public attitude toward unions in Chapter 5.) In the next two chapters I will explore these obstacles to doctors' unions—the question of strikes or job actions in Chapter 3 and the relationship between unionism and professionalism in Chapter 4.

❡ 3 ❡

Physicians' Strikes
in the United States
and Elsewhere

This chapter will look at two doctors' strikes in the United States and several in Canada, Western Europe, and Israel. It will briefly describe the doctors' unions and bargaining arrangements in those countries, and then compare the different frameworks that have made physicians' unions more acceptable in Europe.

Doctors' Strikes in the United States

The record of job actions by small groups of physicians is difficult to trace in the United States. There is no central organization that follows such events. Actions such as the 1973 "white-in" in Nevada, discussed in the previous chapter, which the medical press treated as highly newsworthy at the time, may not find their way into any other larger record. Full-blown physicians' strikes, which have a far better chance of being documented, have been rare in the United States, partly because only a small proportion of doctors have a forum for organizing collective action. On the other hand, doctors have participated in job actions without the aid of organizational structures.

The UAPD has not sponsored a strike in the twenty years of its existence. According to Executive Director Gary Robinson, a strike indicates failure.[1] A union that does its job should be able to prevent the escalation of problems into strikes. Of course, exceptions do

---

[1] Robinson's statements are from interviews conducted in spring 1992.

occur. Robinson says the UAPD came close to calling a strike in 1986.

> The fact that we didn't is miraculous. The county (San Mateo) didn't want to give anything. They tried a lot of tricks. They gave doctors raises without telling us. They gave the interns and residents raises to get rid of them, without telling us.
>
> So eventually, instead of getting everybody on their side, we were able to turn this kind of thing against them. In order to get the union out, they promised the doctors that they would get us decertified and give them more money. There was no way they would give them that money—they were promising big money. We won the election. We said to them, now you've got their expectations up. We expected a 5 percent increase. But they got them up to 20 percent, so we bargained for 20 percent and got it.

While the UAPD did not initiate it, the union did become involved in the single largest strike to date by physicians in private practice in the United States (Pantell and Irwin, 1979). It took place in California in 1975. The job action was precipitated by a combination of things, but the final straw was the increase in the malpractice premium rate announced by insurance carriers in April 1975: 500 percent in southern California and 350 percent in northern California (Cunningham, 1975; Gamble, 1976). The average increase was 486 percent statewide. The premium hike came in the wake of legislative initiatives announced by Governor Jerry Brown. His seven new pieces of legislation were designed to achieve greater state control over licensure, recertification, bed capacity, duplication of services, and binding arbitration of malpractice suits.

In May 1975, anesthesiologists in San Francisco walked out for four weeks. This virtually eliminated elective surgery. Hospital bed occupancy dropped by 50 percent, 40 percent of hospital employees were laid off, and hospital losses were estimated at $7.5 million.

Individuals, rather than a union or any other organized group, were responsible for the strike. The California Medical Association, following the lead of the American Medical Association, took the position that withholding of services by individual physicians did not constitute a strike. Under the circumstances, withholding services was a legitimate way to resolve the dispute over professional issues. Physicians who participated in the walk-out announced their respective decisions as individual responses to the increase in malpractice rates.

In the face of the problems caused by the anesthesiologists' action, the trustees of the California Medical Association volunteered to participate in talks with the State Assembly. Some of those involved in the walk-out asked the UAPD to act as a mediator, in recognition of its negotiating experience. Local newspapers gave the UAPD much of the credit for negotiating a settlement, which ended that June. The situation was, however, far from fully resolved. A second wave of strike actions took place later that year, beginning in December and continuing into February (Gamble, 1976:62), involving a broader range of specialists. During the first phase, 83 hospitals were involved; during the second, 115 hospitals were affected.

In response to continued expressions of readiness to strike on the part of the UAPD membership, union staff members began organizing a statewide strike during the early autumn. The date set was January 1, 1976, the date the premium increase was scheduled to take effect. The union sent 40,000 letters with a strike ballot to all the physicians in the state. The results were reported in the UAPD's December newsletter: 20,000 doctors returned their ballots, voting 2 to 1 to strike. The strike being organized by the UAPD was avoided when the state legislature intervened to bring the parties together to negotiate a more permanent settlement, which was the outcome the UAPD had been advocating. The legislature agreed to review the factors promoting the rise in rates, to consider legislation aimed at curbing escalating premiums, and, most importantly from the point of view of doctors, to do so in cooperation with the medical community.

Another noteworthy strike occurred on the opposite coast within the next three years, in April 1978, against the Group Health Association HMO in Washington, D.C. (Coyne, 1980). The strike was important because GHA was not only a large and well-established HMO; it was also the single largest trade association representing the managed care industry. The organizing impetus which brought GHA into existence had come from organized labor.

The physicians affiliated with GHA had been trying to find a mechanism to use in negotiations with the board over income and conditions of work. They formed a bargaining council. When the National Labor Relations Board determined that the council was an illegal "company union," the physicians started proceedings to incorporate themselves. They emulated the model developed by the physicians affiliated with the largest HMO in the country, Kaiser Permanente. The GHA board voted not to cooperate with such an entity.

The physicians decided that they had no alternative but to establish a union, which they did in 1978. By this time the relationship between the doctors and the board had become so acrimonious that negotiations scheduled for the end of that year had little chance of success. The union offered to accept only a 4 percent increase over the next three years in recognition of GHA's deficits, if the physicians were allowed to see private patients. The GHA refused to consider the outside practice clause. The reaction of the physicians was that "the GHA did not care if they worked as checkers in the A&P after hours or if they boogied until five in the morning. Why should they care if the physicians did something more professional with their time after working hours?" (Coyne, 1980:60). This was the critical issue that precipitated the strike. Negotiations did not resume until the union called in the Federal Mediation and Conciliation Service.

Job Actions in Other Countries

Because doctors in most other industrial countries (and many less developed ones) bargain collectively, their negotiations and job actions have a greater chance of becoming a matter of public record. However, they too must be noteworthy to receive more than passing attention. One cross-cultural literature search produced references, not always full accounts, to 30 strikes that have taken place since 1894 (Antonovsky, 1989).[2] The doctors' strikes in selected countries

[2] To the best of my knowledge, Antonovsky's review of the literature on doctors' strikes stands as the only attempt to produce a comprehensive record. Collecting information on doctors' strikes in other countries is difficult because references often appear only in passing and assume knowledge of the larger social and institutional context. My review here is limited to reports in the English-language press.

discussed here are not necessarily representative of physicians' job actions more generally.

Canada: Canadian physicians' negotiations take place in public, and public opinion plays a large role in their resolution. The first important recorded strike in Canada took place in Saskatchewan in 1962, in response to a major reorganization of the health care delivery system (Blakeney, 1993; Badgley and Wolfe, 1967). The newly installed socialist provincial government initiated plans to make health care services available to all citizens of the province under a government health plan.

Saskatchewan doctors held a mass meeting in May 1962 and agreed to close their offices as of July 1, when the plan was scheduled to go into effect. According to Allan Blakeney, a member of the Saskatchewan legislature at the time, the doctors said they would not withhold emergency care but would do no routine care.

> There was a little bit of hardball for about seventeen days, and then the "emergency services" got better and better. It seems the striking doctors were considering more and more ailments to be "emergencies."
>
> We knew it would be tough, but it was July and people don't get sick much in July. They go on holidays. As a matter of fact, a lot of the doctors went on holiday, too. They said: "Okay, we'll wait two or three weeks and see how things are going. We don't mind being out of our offices a few weeks in July. Who would? This thing has got to settle." (1993:76)

The strike lasted 23 days. The fact that the proposed plan was popular with the public defeated the strikers, in spite of their appeals to professionalism and predictions of dire effects on the doctor-patient relationship. Over the next ten years the plan was extended to all the provinces with no protest from doctors there.

Virtually all physicians in Quebec belong to a union; they have been organized into two unions since 1967, one for family practice physicians and one for specialists. Those two unions staged a one-day "show of solidarity" in 1980 by withholding their services. Ninety-five percent voted in favor of striking, to protest a bill that would have instituted increased controls over medicine (Lefton, 1981b; Bieler, 1981). The high level of solidarity in the one-day strike was apparently unusual. Since the two groups of physicians compete for resources, they generally do not present a united front in bargaining with the provincial government. They did not win very much in this case. Clearly, the two groups would achieve greater bargaining power by joining forces to establish a single union.

Even though they are not unionized, Ontario physicians managed to stage a highly visible and memorable strike in 1986. The strike was a protest against the federal government's decision to outlaw "balance billing," the extra fee that some physicians were charging over and above the amount the government would pay. This strike lasted 25 days. However, as one physician observer points out: "There were many physicians who claimed to be on strike—yet, if you were to go examine their billings over the strike period, you would find, although they may have been out carrying placards part of the time, they were still delivering care to their patients. . . . I think that strike was more of a media event than a real event" (Estill, 1993:46).

In the early 1980s the Canadian Medical Association seriously considered becoming a union (Lefton, 1981a). It ended up deciding not to, but took steps to give itself more bargaining power. The CMA established contingency plans for engaging in collective bargaining, without changing its official status as a professional association. This does not mean that the question of unionization has been settled. The question of changing identity comes up periodically in discussions among members of the various provincial medical associations.

Physicians in all the provinces already engage in negotiations with their respective provincial governments over fees and conditions of work. With the exception of Quebec, the provincial medical societies identify themselves, and are chartered, as professional societies rather than unions. The tough stance taken by provincial governments over the last few years on budget tightening is, however, causing the provincial societies to talk about unionization and strikes once again. Bitter disputes, which have not led to action, have been reported across the country (Meyer, 1992; McCormick, 1993a).

Doctors in British Columbia, for example, say that the provincial government took a "take-it-or-leave-it" stance in developing its budget without traditional bargaining. According to the president of the British Columbia Medical Association (BCMA), most other provinces have created a dispute-resolution mechanism. Until 1993, B.C. physicians did not think they needed such a mechanism. The relationship between doctors and politicians fell apart in 1992 when the provincial government enacted new health legislation permitting it to set a reimbursement cap unilaterally. The BCMA president argued that the association had been functioning as a union for the last twenty years and that formalizing that status would bring added bargaining advantages. For instance, the membership could then employ the formal mediation process under Canadian labor law. In the end, B.C. physicians chose not to turn the medical association into a union, nor did they strike. However, they have made clear that they consider both to be viable options (McCormick, 1993a).

Germany: Over the last decade or so, the German health care system has attracted nearly as much interest in the American academic and trade press as has the Canadian system. Thus we know a great deal about its origins and subsequent difficulties. We know that German doctors organized themselves into a militant labor union in 1898 because they considered their professional association to be insufficiently aggressive (Stone, 1980; Light and Schuller, 1986; Inglehart, 1991; Roemer, 1991). By 1919 approximately 90 percent had joined the union. They registered their dissatisfaction with their working arrangements by striking, up to 200 times a year during the union's earliest years (Light, 1986; Stone, 1980).

They struck in response to what they considered the arbitrary reimbursement practices of sickness funds (the health insurance divisions of the mutual benefit plans created by workers' guilds to provide financial aid to individual members in times of need. This is not surprising, since, when health insurance for workers was initially required by law in 1881, the 22,000 funds of varying sizes began to hire physicians as employees under widely varying conditions. Some were poorly managed and, because of underfunding, did not always pay doctors what they had agreed (Inglehart, 1991). The fact that doctors were hired by the blue-collar managers of the funds, whose status was lower than that of physicians, was another persistent source of irritation (Stone, 1980).

Over time the situation became more settled, with the most extensive change occurring during the Nazi era (Liebfried and Tennstedt, 1986). The number of funds began to decline during this period; as of 1991 there were 1,147 (Inglehart, 1991). It was during the 1930s and 1940s that the funds began transferring responsibility for issuing reimbursements to bargaining units associated with the local medical societies, the country-level insurance doctors associations (Godt, 1987). Once these local insurance associations became well established, the number of strikes diminished. Individual physicians who had complaints about reimbursements could then take them to a board of colleagues. This board was authorized to require physicians to explain exceptionally high bills.

Representatives of the insurance associations negotiate with the sickness funds to establish an annual budget. The funds are responsible for collecting the money to cover health care costs. The medical society is responsible for keeping reimbursements under the allotted budget. Both participate in decisions to raise employer/employee contributions and to revise services. Such changes are overseen by the federal government, which has an interest in containing costs.

The government's role deserves special attention. It acts as coordinator of interest groups that vie with each other for national resources. The stance taken by both the government and doctors reflects the larger system of values in Germany. Deborah Stone writes: "In Germany, the medical profession has been allowed to regulate itself because the dominant ideology holds that all important social and economic functions are best performed by self-regulatory corporative groups" (1980:163).

Societal commitment to the idea that the government is responsible for achieving a balance of interests does not mean that any particular group will be completely satisfied with the solutions the government advocates. In 1992 doctors protested the severely restrictive reforms instituted by the government in the wake of a 10 percent rise in costs during the preceding year (Meyer, 1993c). The measures included a global budget on pharmaceuticals; a ceiling on payments tied to wage growth and expected to be 3 to 4 percent; mandatory retirement by age 68; a 10 percent cut in dental prosthetic care; and some cost-sharing by patients. Dentists staged a strike and physicians had patients sign petitions, but the public generally supported the reforms and the government did not back down.

Sweden and Denmark: American scholars have been interested in Scandinavian health care systems for many years largely because their health statistics have been so impressive (Anderson, 1972). Doctors in Sweden, Denmark, Finland, and Norway all engage in collective bargaining and have done so for as long as anyone can remember.

Traditionally, most Danish doctors have worked in private practice, receiving reimbursements from sickness funds. By contrast, in Sweden a high proportion of doctors traditionally entered salaried practice (Carder and Klingeberg, 1980; Ito, 1980). Those who practiced outside the major cities were willing to work on a salaried basis both because rural areas were too sparsely populated to provide a secure income and because the county governments insisted on greater predictability of health care costs. Thus, when the government put pressure on urban doctors to move toward salaried practice during the 1970s as a cost containment measure, doctors were familiar with such arrangements and the majority agreed to do so without much protest. In fact, they rarely find it necessary to resort to militant tactics even though 94 percent belong to unions (Saltman, 1990).

However, both Danish and Swedish doctors struck in 1981. The strikes were precipitated by disputes over on-call remuneration for hospital based doctors, especially the junior doctors (Heindenheimer and Johansen, 1985). The resolution in Sweden resulted in increased government control and a smaller number of positions for junior doctors. In Denmark the dispute was "more dramatic, more irregular and more unpredictable." It also produced a "spectacular increase" in the number of jobs for younger doctors and increased expenditures.

Heindenheimer and Johansen attribute the difference in outcomes to the negotiation process and the structure of the organizations involved. The process was well established and routinized in Sweden, in sharp contrast to Denmark, where county-level planning and negotiating arrangements instituted after the elimination of the sickness funds during the mid-1970s were not yet fully regularized. Competition among the three professional associations representing

Danish physicians added to the complexity of the negotiations. Swedish doctors, on the other hand, are represented by a single association that operates within the framework of a larger labor union. The massive strike staged by Swedish doctors in 1986 attracted the attention of the American medical press. The strike was in response to government efforts to decrease wage differentials across occupations (Weisman, 1987). The strike lasted three and a half weeks, involved 10 percent of all Swedish physicians, and closed 15 of Sweden's 100 hospitals. Doctors argued that their purchasing power had declined by 30 percent over the last ten years because the Social Democrats and the largest and most powerful blue collar unions were intent on decreasing wage differences across occupational groups. When it appeared that the government was ready to agree to the doctors' demands that they should be given special consideration, the members of four unions mounted a protest strike. They included nurses, nurses' aides, telephone operators, and weather forecasters. The protest strikers did not gain the public's support. The strike was settled when the government agreed to an increase of 7.4 percent for all workers involved, plus a $9 million lump sum for those in the health and social welfare professions (Weisman, 1987:33).

Israel: Israeli doctors participated in notable strikes in 1973, 1976, and 1983 (Harrison, 1991; Antonovsky, 1989). Compared to other industrial nations, both the frequency and intensity of strike activity were high during the late 1970s and early 1980s, when Israel was experiencing a high rate of inflation (Harrison, 1991). It was especially prevalent among public and semi-public employees. Doctors' strikes were in response to the same realities.

The 1983 strike was the most militant. It involved 8,000 doctors from all parts of the country and lasted four months. It began with a three-day walk-out by almost all physicians in the country, with the exception of the few who kept emergency rooms functioning. By the end of the strike period, some doctors had begun a hunger strike. Since virtually all Israeli doctors belonged to a union, they had a forum for establishing a consensus on strike conditions. They agreed to provide emergency services and care for some frail and all elderly patients. The strike lasted so long because they did not fear reprisals, the public was generally supportive, and the strike was blamed on the intransigence of the government. The strike ended when the government relented and agreed to meet at least some of the doctors' demands.

United Kingdom: Although the British Medical Association (BMA) turned itself into a union in 1974, it had been acting in this capacity for much longer. The BMA has been engaged in collective bargaining with the government since the turn of the century, more so since 1948 when the National Health Service, the current health care delivery system, was fully implemented. The decision to change its status formally was prompted by a change in labor legislation in 1971. According to a representative of the BMA: "The BMA has evolved for its own purposes a style of trade unionism that meets doctors' needs, takes account of their professional and ethical standards, and is quite distinctive from the 'industrial unionism' that most doctors firmly shunned" (Ellis, 1982). The BMA has also been prepared to use job actions as well as all other channels of influence available to it (Lumley, 1973).

While British doctors do engage in job actions, these activities do not seem to warrant much comment. What tends to receive more attention is doctors' concern about the extent to which their professionalism is being affected by government efforts to change the structure of the National Health Service (Harrison, 1988). One observer, writing about Australian doctors, concludes that in modeling themselves after their British colleagues, "they are content to debate their professionalism" (Willis, 1988).

Cross-Cultural Values and Doctors' Strikes

This review of doctors' strikes makes clear that doctors' unions are products of their societies. Whether unions are militant or conciliatory depends upon the larger context of social understandings and expectations that characterize the society that spawns them. While doctors, whether unionized or not, may resort to job actions to express exceptional levels of frustration, on the whole, physicians' unions tend to be conciliatory. To the extent that the militant behavior of doctors' unions cross-culturally reveals any patterns, it appears that doctors' strikes are more likely to erupt during periods of change and in response to changes that doctors consider unfair. What constitutes "unfair" is, of course, relative and culture-bound. Doctors engage in job actions usually in response to major shifts in prevailing arrangements, even more so when they feel that their views are not adequately represented.

There also seems to be a pattern indicating when militancy will pay off (Cohn, 1993): when the public supports the doctors' position. Without public support, doctors' strikes generally do not succeed.[3]

The number of doctors' strikes has been high during the 1980s because health care systems throughout the industrialized world were undergoing significant changes in response to similar pressures—technological innovation, rising expectations on the part of patients, aging of the population, and the rising costs these trends produced (Dohler, 1989; Godt, 1987; Spek, 1980). The reforms introduced in many countries had significant consequences for doctors. Canada, for example, instituted universal coverage and established collective bargaining for doctors during this period. Most countries achieved resolutions that were widely supported by the public and accepted, if not always enthusiastically, by doctors.

The United States began the process of health care reform during that era as well, by introducing two massive health insurance programs, Medicare and Medicaid. (I discuss the social context in which this occurred in Chapter 5.) The AMA actively protested the reforms, which were enacted because the public favored them. The programs stand as monuments to the American value system and in stark contrast to the values governing the reforms introduced in other industrialized countries during the same period.

Americans, then and now, are expected to obtain health insurance on an individual basis through employment. This does not make the United States unique; many other countries have systems based partly on employment. What is special is the notion that those who fail to obtain insurance via employment may not be "deserving." The result is that the services included and the guidelines governing eligibility for coverage by public programs are a source of continuing debate, focusing on whether particular categories of persons are truly deserving of publicly supported health care.

---

[3] For a more extended discussion of the role of public opinion, see Lomas and Constandriopoulos, who call it "one of the key instruments" in battles between physicians and governments (1994:256).

Such debates produce insecurity and frustration for individuals whose coverage might be cut, providers (doctors, hospitals, and health care workers) whose bills might not be paid, taxpayers who are told they are paying for excessive and unnecessary services, and politicians whose opponents blame them for being negligent about monitoring rising costs.

When such debates become especially heated, doctors end up being blamed for rising costs and other problems in the system. After all, it is said, they are the ones who order the costly services. Given the complexity of health care delivery arrangements and all the factors that have led to rising costs, doctors are understandably unwilling to accept total responsibility for this or other problems. In fact, according to Dr. Marcus, being targeted unfairly is what upsets doctors most. Antonovsky reached the same conclusion after reviewing doctors' strikes in Israel and elsewhere (1989:313).

Until the early 1970s, American physicians expressed little interest in organizing themselves to take a collective stance because they could rely on their claim to a high level of professionalism and the generous rewards this produced. This stance was (and continues to be) consistent with the social values to which Americans are committed. Professionalism is sustained by the larger system of values that prevails in the United States. In other industrialized countries, politicized labor movements challenge the notion that most citizens can be classified as middle-class. Professionals in those countries depend less on an ideology of professionalism to legitimate their claims to greater social and economic rewards; they are forthright about using labor organizations (Larson, 1977). Given the American value system, physicians' unions in the United States face a major contradiction in calling for collective action. Collective action promises collective gain, which is inconsistent with the dominant social ideology. Individual worth in this society is measured in terms of individual achievement and individual solutions.

The American value system is also incompatible with social concern about rising health care costs. It is difficult to see how doctors who are being pressed to assume greater responsibility over health care costs can do so unless they agree to do so collectively (Lomas and Constandriopoulos, 1994). It has been easier to fulfill social expectations of high-quality care within the framework of individualism than it will be to fulfill the more recent expectations of cost effectiveness.

In sum, American doctors' resistance to physicians' unions has been, and continues to be, grounded in the larger system of social values. The dominant value system supports the individualistic compulsion to prove oneself worthy based on one's individual achievements, a compulsion which is not satisfied through collective victory. Medical professionalism has been so successful because it permitted individual differentiation and defended conditions which preserved the autonomy of individual practitioners. It has been supportive of the social conditions that produced deference and compliance in personal interaction with individual members of the profession even as it denied the existence of structural inequality. As Dr. Marcus points out, however, professionalism has not been producing nearly as much deference in recent years as it did in the past, and high income is simply not a sufficiently satisfying reward.

This is undoubtedly not what Dr. Michael Halberstam (quoted in the last chapter) had in mind when he charged that physicians' unions are unprofessional. In the next chapter I examine what doctors and others mean when they invoke the concept of professionalism.

❧ 4 ❧

Professionalism:
Construction of the Concept

One of the themes to which Dr. Marcus repeatedly returns in his recruitment efforts is "professionalism." He consistently castigates his colleagues for their attachment to rhetoric rather than reality.

> With the forces that are arrayed against him it becomes certain that without vigorous representation of his rights by forces that have been conspicuously lacking in the past, the physician must certainly be reduced to the level of a public functionary, accorded no more respect or status than the poor postal employees or public-school teachers in *their* pre-union days. It is fatuous and vain to hope that the value of the physician to society should be self-evident. All his posturing about professionalism becomes tragicomical when idols are toppling all around him. If he indeed feels pride in the dignity and achievements of his profession he is being called upon for the first time in history to exemplify that pride through concrete action rather than lofty rhetoric. With nostalgia for the good old days, but imbued with the pragmatic realization that *none* of his values can otherwise be preserved, he is reluctantly entering the Age of Medical Unionization. (1978:38)

Dr. Marcus's message is unmistakable: the language and imagery of professionalism no longer serve the purpose they did in the past, namely, to convince society that the medical profession deserves society's trust. He argues that the rhetoric is not only empty but dysfunctional. It prevents physicians from facing the reality of the situation in which they now collectively find themselves. In order to appreciate the strength of the sentiments underlying this argument, I will examine what professionalism means both to those who assign the label and to those who claim it.

Professionalism has attracted the attention of scholars over the last three quarters of the century. Medicine has consistently received more attention than other occupations both because of its success in having its claims acknowledged and because of the high level of reward it was able to garner as a result. But over the last decade or two, according to many observers, medicine's ability to assert its professionalism and to enjoy the rewards thereof has been slipping.[1] This chapter describes different views of the functions of medical professionalism over the years. The purpose is to provide a context for discussing the charge made repeatedly by critics of the physicians' union movement—that there is an insurmountable conflict between professionalism and unionism.

The meaning of professionalism evolved over the past two centuries from sacred vocation to secular occupational identity (Kimball, 1992). During the nineteenth and most of the twentieth centuries, taking up a profession was the socially approved route to middle-class status (Berlant, 1975; Geisen, 1983). Samuel Haber puts it this way: a profession in the eighteenth century was an occupation that a gentleman could take up "without demeaning himself, and more wondrously, an occupation that might make someone a gentleman simply by his taking it up" (1991, preface). Striving for middle-class status required that individuals, and eventually whole occupational groups, present themselves as sober, hardworking, trustworthy, and well educated, that is to say, gentlemanly in all aspects of their behavior.

The promise to conform to such middle-class values carried the implicit promise that the occupational group would oversee members' work, in order to protect the public from the few who might be tempted to engage in illegal or immoral practices. Professional

---

[1] Evidence comes from the Confidence in Social Institutions survey data presented in Chapter 5, as well as surveys reviewed by Blendon and Altman (1984). Scholars who have commented on the trend include, among others, Hafferty and McKinlay, 1993; and Levy, 1991. See also the entire issue of the *Milbank Quarterly*, 1988, vol. 66, Supplement 2.

credentials were offered as confirmation of the individual's "inner character" (Bledstein, 1976). In return, gentlemen expected reasonably secure incomes that would permit them comfortable life styles.[2]

Viewing professionalism in this light puts into better perspective social scientists' preoccupation during earlier decades of this century with identifying the occupational characteristics that differentiated the professions from other occupations.[3] Most social scientists offered no opinion on the prevailing social attitude that held successful professionalization of an occupation in high regard. However, a small number took clear positions on the social implications of professionalism; it is their views that I have selected to outline here.

The Social Functions of Medical Professionalism

Regardless of their attitudes toward the social value of professionalism, virtually all scholars agree that medicine was particularly successful in convincing society that medical professionalism was socially desirable. They also agree that physicians succeeded in achieving a monopoly over the knowledge base of medical science and an exclusive right to apply or oversee the application of that knowledge (Hafferty, 1988). Beyond this, the consensus falls apart. Considerable disagreement exists about the impact on society of the pursuit of professionalism.

Talcott Parsons's work occupies the positive end of the spectrum (1951). He portrayed the socially advantaged status achieved by medicine as highly functional, that is, beneficial to society. According to Parsons, doctors worked to improve the health of patients, which insured that those patients would be able to perform their

---

[2] It must be noted that such assessments inspired a few observers to offer the following corrective: that it was the social elite, as opposed to society as a whole, that was interested in promoting professionalism, including medical professionalism (McKinlay and Arches, 1985). Furthermore, this was true only because the social values associated with professionalism happened to coincide with the needs of the capitalist class (Berlant, 1975; Navarro, 1986).

[3] Reviews of the sociological literature, at least the more extensive ones, begin by outlining Max Weber's observations linking the emergence of professionalism to broader social trends including bureaucratization, rationalism, and capitalism (Ritzer and Walczak, 1986, 1988). Shorter reviews generally begin with the works of scholars who wrote during the 1930s (for an overview see Hall, 1975; Perrow, 1986; Ritzer and Walczak, 1986).

respective roles, thus insuring social stability and order. For this, physicians deserved to be generously rewarded. The characteristics associated with the role served to protect society.[4]

Parsons did recognize, however, the risks inherent in the role. Indeed, the potential for deviance was clearly his central concern. He recognized that individual doctors were in a position to take advantage of individual patients; patients are vulnerable because they must reveal extensive personal information and follow doctors' orders in order to get well. Patients must interact with physicians when they are especially susceptible to influence—when in pain and fearful of the consequences of illness. Parsons recognized that physicians could take economic advantage of patients under such conditions; however, he was apparently more concerned about the psycho-social risks involved. Parsons focused on the fact that physicians could take sexual advantage or exercise a hold over patients who revealed secrets to them. The value he attached to social stability meant that he was interested in mechanisms of social control that would prevent such deviance.[5]

Parsons's concern about the effectiveness of social control over medicine reflects an important characteristic of the physician's role at the time he was making these observations (Rueschemeyer, 1983). In 1951, most physicians were engaged in solo private practice. In fact, this pattern remained intact well into the second half of the twentieth century. Physicians worked in small and scattered offices, behind closed doors, often with only a receptionist or a nurse to assist them. These are the structural characteristics that prevented a more systematic or bureaucratic system of control from being imposed. They are also the circumstances that caused professionalism to become established as the primary form of social control over medical work.

---

[4] According to Parsons, doctors were expected to observe a " 'professional' pattern" of social norms governing their behavior. These include a record of achieved technical competence; universalism in treating patients rather than showing a preference for some; affective neutrality rather than emotional involvement with patients; and functional specificity, requiring them to limit their advice to the medical realm rather than offering generalized wisdom.

[5] Parsons devotes an entire chapter to the problems associated with social control in *The Social System* (Glencoe, Ill.: Free Press, 1951).

From Parsons's perspective, the powerful norms governing professional behavior were society's best chance of instituting controls over the doctor-patient interactions that took place under these special conditions. Patients really had few alternatives but to invest their trust in the physician. Asking for a second opinion was frowned upon until relatively recently, viewed as an insulting expression of distrust that would damage the doctor-patient relationship. Furthermore, it was customary for general practitioners to provide a full range of health care services. As a result, patients were less apt to be referred to other physicians, that is, to specialists.

In effect, medical professionalism evolved as the primary means of social control over doctors because there were no viable alternatives. Physicians embraced it because it assured them a great deal of individual autonomy. In return, they were prepared to promise that they would continually strive to improve quality and monitor the performance of fellow physicians. Professionalism evolved as a powerful symbolic shield against medical deviance. Whether society was duped in believing medicine's promises remains a matter of debate, but that society extended a broad social mandate to medicine based on assurance of professionalism is indisputable (Hughes, 1957).

The Conflict Model of Medical Professionalism

Although Parsons may have been concerned about the risk of individual patients' being economically exploited by individual physicians, he did not express much interest in the risk that the profession as a whole would seek to take economic advantage of its position. Few other scholars raised this concern during the first seven decades of the century, at least not in a way that would capture public interest (Rayack, 1967; Shryrock, 1947). However, this was exactly the concern expressed by those who wrote after 1970, and this time the concern did capture the public's attention. Interest now turned to *how* physicians achieved their advantaged position.

Eliot Freidson's book *Professional Dominance* signaled the turning point in society's readiness to accept the view that the medical profession had acted in self-interest rather than patients' interests. His analysis of the relationship between physicians and patients was quickly embraced and widely disseminated. This perspective was consistent with the growing sense that medicine had ignored the inequities in the system of health care delivery, catering to those who had the resources to pay for care and largely disregarding the needs of the poor. This was not, of course, a new observation. The same critique had been made by various commissions constituted to study health care delivery arrangements during earlier decades. The difference between the late 1960s and preceding decades was that the observations suddenly captured the attention of the general public (Budrys, 1986).

Freidson's work opened the door to the power or conflict theory of the impact of medical professionalism on society. This theory holds that medicine achieved its status and power by monopolizing control over medical work, by eliminating competition from other occupational groups and institutionalizing this achievement in medical practice act legislation, that is, licensure (for review see Halmos, 1973; Ritzer, and Walczak, 1986). Physicians were now held responsible for having encouraged client dependence and passivity (Bledstein, 1976); physicians who said they were merely responding to clients' requests and widespread social needs were said to be justifying their self-serving behavior (McKinlay, 1973).

The picture painted by this new wave of theorists moved rapidly from the realm of academic discussion to the platform of public policy debate among activists. The conflict view provided the basis for devising policies aimed at correcting the flaws in the health care delivery system which, proponents argued, had resulted from medicine's self-interested agenda. Policy makers advocated mechanisms to give more control to the public, that is, potential patients. These ideas were well received by society because they were consistent with the revolution in attitude toward the whole range of social institutions that was emerging at this time. The popularity of the message is borne out by the volume of legislation designed to impose public control that was passed during the 1960s and early 1970s (outlined in Chapter 5). Physicians were, of course, fully aware of this dramatic shift in social attitude. Indeed, it is during this period, the early 1970s, that the physicians' union movement erupted on the scene.

Why the Changing Interpretation?

The shift in thinking about the value of medical professionalism is due at least in part to changes in the larger social context. Theo-

rists saw the same occupation so differently because they were ob-
serving it during distinctly different periods. The functionalists' position is framed by a view of society that is orderly and stable—a
representation that predates the social upheavals of the late 1960s.
This is also the period to which physicians nostalgically refer as the
"Golden Age of Medicine" (Burnham, 1982; Light and Levine, 1988;
Gray, 1991; Larkin, 1993). After the 1960s, society was more often
portrayed as conflictual and as intentionally structured to benefit
those who were already disproportionately advantaged.

Each perspective reflects the social context prevailing at the time
in which it was presented. The functionalists were interested in identifying the characteristics that distinguished the medical profession
from other occupations because the process leading to successful
professionalization per se, not only in medicine, was itself valued.
The conflict theorists focused on the mechanisms medicine had employed to attain its socially advantaged position at a time when social
inequality was being identified as a critical factor responsible for the
prevailing social disorder.

The shifts in thinking about medicine over the last 30 years have
not been easy for members of the medical profession to understand.
At the same time, the occupation itself was changing drastically—
becoming more internally diversified (Abbott, 1988; DeSantis,
1980). Furthermore, the settings in which medical work was being
performed were becoming more centralized and coming under the
control of increasingly larger organizations. In combination, these
two trends have made it far more difficult to identify solutions that
the majority of physicians could support and that would satisfy the
public.

As Dr. Marcus saw it in the early 1970s, doctors were turning to
outdated definitions of medical professionalism to avoid admitting
that their professional prerogatives were actually at risk. Before focusing on the UAPD's response to the organizational challenge inherent in this scenario, let us examine the changes that took place in
the health sector during the 1970s—changes that doctors considered
so objectionable that unionism suddenly seemed an acceptable approach.

⚑ 5 ⚐

The End of the
Golden Age

The sudden eruption of discontent among physicians and their unlikely readiness to consider unionization were a response to the social changes of the early 1970s. To understand doctors' reactions, one must view the changes in health care delivery arrangements from their perspective. In their view, the changes signaled the end of the Golden Age of Medicine (Burnham, 1982; Light and Levine, 1988; Greco and Eisenberg, 1993; Larkin, 1993).

Dr. Marcus outlined the sense of loss that doctors were experiencing in a 1975 article:

> The physician as healer has been accorded a place of respect and esteem by the very nature of the service he rendered— personal concern, amelioration of suffering, quasi-mystical intervention in the struggle between life and inevitability of death, these were his stock in trade. There was the tacit acceptance of the fact that he should be accorded a special niche in society, measured both by the honor it accorded him and by a standard of living that was reasonably expected to be somewhat above others whose responsibilities were less than his. His long years of training, hours of service, risk of exposure to disease, shortened earning life-span, attenuated freedom and family life, and devotion to professional self-advancement all seemed to justify a special status. In return, the American medical profession developed a high standard of medical care that was unequaled anywhere in the world, indeed a fair exchange, it would seem. (1975b:37–38)

The climate of social change and experimentation that characterized the 1960s fostered the emergence of new organizations and
agencies in the health sector. In Dr. Marcus's view, this amounted to
"all sorts of forces interposing themselves" between physicians and
patients. Moreover, these interlopers were gaining so much power
that the medical establishment's power was being diminished: "The
old-line medical organizations have been powerless to impress upon
insurance companies, hospital administration, and certainly government, the fact that physicians . . . are no longer able to play a dominant role in the determination of their professional lives or liveli-
hoods" (1978:38).

Dr. Marcus warned his colleagues of the imminent disastrous
changes that would be caused by government's expanding role in the
organization of health care delivery. He chided them for ignoring
this obvious new reality and choosing, instead, to hide behind their
professionalism:

> No amount of preening and posturing under the banner of
> "professionalism" will countervail the inevitability of govern-
> ment-financed medicine. . . . But it is as certain as tomorrow's
> sunrise that faceless cost-accountants, issuing decrees from the
> Dept. of HEW, will determine the modalities of medical care in
> the United States within the next two or three years. (1973:5)

He concluded that such changes signaled the emergence of a
"Brave New World of Medicine" that would leave doctors with no
alternative but to enter, albeit reluctantly, into the Age of Medical
Unionization.

While only a relatively small proportion of doctors were prepared to join a union, there was growing consensus that their control
over the practice of medicine was being ripped away (Gray, 1991).
They agreed that the government was the main source of their problems. Paul Starr described doctors' changing situation: "The sover-
eignty of the medical profession entailed the restriction of competition, the limiting of regulation by government or private
organizations, and authority to define and interpret the standards
and the understandings that govern medical work. Emerging devel-

opments now jeopardize the profession's control of markets, organizations, and standards of judgement" (1982:421).

Doctors were losing their mandate to organize the delivery of care as they saw fit. According to Starr:

> Previously, two premises had guided government health policy: first, that Americans needed more medical care—more than the market alone would provide; and second, that medical professionals and private voluntary institutions were best equipped to decide how to organize those services. Until the 1970s the first of these premises had not yet undermined the second. Increased federal aid initially did not much enlarge the scope of public regulation. Practitioners, hospitals, researchers, and medical schools enjoyed a broad grant of authority to run their own affairs. (1982:379)

The system of health care delivery was now evolving without medicine's input and often in contradiction to its stated preferences. The fact that physicians were not alone in their frustration about the direction of change did not ameliorate the situation. It did not help to know that the shift from trust to distrust of medical professionals was the product of the larger social awakening that characterized the 1960s.

Many social institutions had become the subject of social scrutiny during the 1960s, and all were found wanting. The "confidence in social institutions" surveys that began in 1966 reflect the citizenry's declining trust across the board. The table on the following page shows the proportion of a national sample of respondents who say they have a "great deal" of confidence in the "people running" various social institutions.[1]

While doctors may have been traumatized by the changes of the late 1960s and early 1970s, medicine as an institution continued to inspire more public confidence than other social institutions. (It maintained this position until 1991, when it fell to second place

---

[1] The question was: "I am going to name some institutions in this country. As far as the *people running* these institutions are concerned, would you say you have a great deal of confidence, only some confidence, or hardly any confidence at all in them?"

Percentage of respondents expressing confidence in social institutions

	1966[a]	1970[a]	1980[b]	1990[b]	1991[b]	1994[b]
Medicine	72 (1)[c]	61	53	46	48	42 (1)
Banks	67 (2)	36	33	18	13	18 (8)
Military	62 (3)	27	29	34	61	38 (3)
Education	61 (4)	37	31	27	31	25.2 (7)
Scientific community	56 (5)	32	46	41	44	41 (2)
Major companies	55 (6)	27	29	26	21	26 (5)
Supreme Court	50 (7)	23	26	37	39	31 (4)
Congress	42 (8)	19	10	16	18	8 (13)
Organized religion	41 (9)	27	38	24	26	24.8 (6)
Executive branch	41 (9)	23	13	24	27	12 (9)
Press	29 (11)	18	23	15	17	9.9 (11)
T.V.	25 (12)	22	16	14	15	9.6 (12)
Organized labor	22 (13)	14	16	11	12	11 (10)

[a] Tom Smith, "Can We Have Confidence in Confidence? Revisited," *Measurement of Subjective Phenomena* (Washington, D.C.: U.S. Bureau of the Census), 1981, pp. 119–189.

[b] James Davis and Tom Smith, "General Social Surveys, 1972–1994: Cumulative Codebook," National Opinion Research Center, University of Chicago, November 1994.

[c] Highest to lowest rankings appear in parentheses.

behind the military, and regained first place in 1994.) The public has been less dissatisfied with and presumably less inclined to demand dramatic changes in medicine than other institutions. Although this brought little solace to physicians at the time (or now), it does put society's view of medicine into perspective.

Various other high-status occupations were registering discontent around this time. In 1972, the American Management Association conducted a survey of managers at 500 companies (DeMaria, Tarnowieski and Gurman, 1972). More than one out of three middle managers who responded indicated willingness to join a managers' union, in hopes of more job security, higher wages, and better benefits.

Social Upheaval and the Demand for Change

The discontent that characterized the late 1960s and early 1970s had its roots in the 1950s and early 1960s, when much, though not all, of society was enjoying steadily increasing prosperity. Prosperity raised expectations, which gave impetus to a wide range of legislative programs. The burst of social legislation enacted during the mid-1960s was a product of President John Kennedy's agenda for social change. That agenda was carried on by President Lyndon Johnson, who declared a "war on poverty," proposed civil rights legislation and inaugurated an ambitious set of health care delivery programs. The social climate of the 1960s was intolerant of promises that would take years to implement. Thus society was not willing to accept medicine's promises to change the health care system by revising the curriculum in medical schools—a measure at improving the performance of the next generation of physicians.

The medical profession was not well equipped to rapidly change the structures it had spent many years creating. The medical establishment was at a loss as to how to respond. Doctors were clearly unwilling to cooperate in restructuring the health care system to meet the newly identified social expectations. Organized medicine was unalterably opposed to the introduction of Medicare and Medicaid, labelling them socialized medicine. The medical establishment predicted that such legislation would result in government interference in the delivery of care, which would lead, in turn, to a steady decline in quality. The campaign left medicine with a tarnished image, as an opponent of proposals the public saw as benefiting the most needy members of society.

Medicine's negative image was reinforced when it became clear that the costs of Medicare and Medicaid were surpassing projections by wide margins. By the end of the first year, it was apparent that the two programs were responsible for a significant increase in utilization of health services, which translated into a steep rise in the government's share of the bill for health care (Stevens, 1989, 1971; Davis and Rowland, 1983). This led to the assessment that the same physicians who had vigorously resisted Medicare and Medicaid were now getting rich from these programs. The fact that the health of society showed no visible sign of improvement added to the public's outrage.

The scholarly literature reflected, perhaps even reinforced, the shift in attitude toward medicine.[2] Social scientists embraced Eliot

[2] The discussion to follow is largely based on Chapters 1–5 in *Planning for the Nation's Health*, Budrys, 1986.

Freidson's analysis of professionalism discussed in the previous chapter, in which he identified the dysfunctional nature of "professional dominance" by physicians (1970a). Policy makers quickly adopted the concept and introduced it to the public. The public responded with a growing demand for patients to have more say in their care. A "health rights movement" appeared on the scene, complete with a "patients' bill of rights." Activists demanded information that would allow patients to make informed choices about care options. Preventive care advice in the media, self-help groups, and living wills all suddenly made their appearance.

The women's movement gave rise to several streams of criticism directed at medicine (Ruzek, 1979). Feminists pointed out the subservient role of female nurses in contrast to the glorified role of male doctors. Feminist scholars made clear that this relationship was not accidental but the result of a long history of male physicians' concerted effort to achieve control over the delivery of health services (Ehrenreich and English, 1973). More outrage grew in the wake of evidence that women were being subjected to treatments that were unnecessary and in some cases detrimental (Ehrenreich and English, 1978; Blaxter, 1983). Such reports, combined with the larger sense that institutions could not be trusted, inspired the groundbreaking 1971 self-help book from the Boston Women's Health Collective, *Our Bodies, Our Selves* (revised in 1992). The Collective wanted to give women power over their health by demystifying physiology and treatment. The message was not subtle. The feminist critique of medicine portrayed doctors as having taken far too much decision-making power over treatment away from patients, specifically female patients, for whom they had little respect and no empathy.

One of the more extreme criticisms to attract popular attention came from Ivan Illich (1976). He popularized the concept of "iatrogenesis," arguing that physicians were doing more to cause disease than to cure it. The fact that this thesis received as much attention as it did is indicative of society's mood.

Organized medicine's reaction to the health rights movement came as a surprise to the public. Most doctors were not enthusiastic about accommodating themselves to greater patient participation in decision-making. Having been the trusted advisors who made decisions in the patients' best interests, they were unaccustomed to the idea that patients needed to participate in a process about which they were not well informed. Educating patients would be time-consuming. And there was the risk that patients would lose confidence in medicine if physicians made clear how tentative the decision-making process was in many instances, and how little knowledge about the disease process they often had available.

Legislative Initiatives

When the Johnson administration proposed a series of far-reaching initiatives intended to bring the public into the decision-making process at the institutional level, the medical establishment campaigned publicly against all of them. Three of Johnson's most noteworthy objectives were eliminating the three killer diseases (heart disease, cancer, and stroke), bringing members of the public into health planning for their own communities, and increasing health manpower.

The Regional Medical Program (RMP) legislation passed in 1967 allocated unprecedented amounts to fight the three killer diseases. The medical community used the funds to create intensive care units that used sophisticated technology to monitor the disease process. While this was not an approach that would produce a victory over the three diseases, it impressed influential members of the public who were in a position to comment on it.

The second major piece of health legislation was designed to give more voice in the operation of health care delivery organizations. A 1967 bill established Comprehensive Health Planning (CHP) agencies. The third initiative, in 1965, appropriated substantial funds to expand health manpower. By the beginning of the 1970s, medical schools could obtain funds from the federal government only by increasing enrollment by 10 percent per year. Even though the impact of this initiative would not be felt for years to come, it was well received by the public.

By the early 1970s it had become clear that the interventions of the 1960s were producing unanticipated consequences, steadily rising costs being the most visible. When analysts sought to find out why, the answers turned out to be complicated and controversial. The negative reactions inspired by medicine's opposition to Medicare and Medicaid did, however, encourage analysts and the public to put greater pressure on medicine to be more socially responsive. The sense that even greater pressure was required was bolstered by early reports on the workings of the RMP and CHP committees. The informal reports indicated that doctors and administrators, now identified as "providers," were dominating decision-making and acting in ways that reduced the influence of the non-medical committee participants, now labeled "consumers."

The lack of evidence of positive effects of the 1960s legislation must have been disappointing to the authors. Policy makers responded by announcing even more extensive legislative reform. Three major correctives were enacted during the early 1970s. First, the PSRO (Professional Standards Review Organizations) legislation was passed in 1972, with the aim of stopping the rise in costs. It discouraged unnecessary services by denying Medicare payment for them. Second, President Nixon initiated legislation to establish prepaid care through HMOs in 1973. By calling the concept "health maintenance" and describing it as focused on preventive care, the Nixon administration overcame the "socialized medicine" label long used by organized medicine to discourage public support.

The views of Paul Ellwood, who was then the primary proponent of health maintenance organizations (and who is now one of the main advocates of the current version—"managed care") attracted much attention from his medical colleagues. It is easy to see how the changes in work arrangements be envisioned would have a chilling effect on doctors. As he foresaw it, HMOs would foster a shift to a free-market economy in which health care services would be "produced" by organizations rather than individuals. This would "stimulate a course of change in the health care industry that would have some of the classical aspects of the industrial revolution—conversion to large units of production, technological innovation, division of labor, substitution of capital for labor, vigorous competition and profitability as the mandatory condition of survival" (Ellwood et al., 1971:298).

The third piece of legislation enacted during this period, the Health Planning and Development Act of 1974, was designed to deal with provider domination of the boards overseeing the Regional Medical Problem and the Comprehensive Health Planning program.

The idea was to give consumers a much stronger voice in health planning. The act mandated a network of health planning agencies, the Health Systems Agencies (HSAs), with consumers allotted the majority of seats. In total 205 such agencies were established. The teeth came from the Certificate of Need (CON) portion of the law, which required hospitals to submit a plan to the agency for review and approval before altering their number of beds or engaging in major expansion.

Although physicians were held responsible for the lack of improvement in the nation's health even as costs were rapidly increasing, doctors were not at all sure what they should or could do about rising costs and utilization of their services. If they used fewer tests, they were certain they could be sued for malpractice. The cost of malpractice insurance was rising astronomically in the early 1970s, reaching an unprecedented level by 1974. Doctors felt they were being unfairly targeted for trends they could not control, and that there was little sense in making individual financial sacrifices by reducing their charges or cutting back on services.

The physicians' union movement was born out of a turbulent social environment. Its growth was fueled by doctors' increasing frustration. The elevated level of frustration could not last, however. As it began to dissipate, so did much of the fervor that gave rise to the union movement. By the end of the decade the physicians' union movement as a whole was faltering. The UAPD, by contrast, continued to grow and become more firmly established, largely because of the organizational decisions made by Dr. Marcus during the union's formative years. I turn to this subject in Chapter 6.

❦ 6 ❧

The Union's
Formative Years

D r. Marcus took up the task of organizing the union methodi-
cally. Once he issued the call and doctors responded, he realized he "had to put up or shut up."[1] He recognized that he could not
do everything himself, so he turned to experienced organizers for
help. He turned first to the leadership of the labor establishment,
calling on George Meany, then the president of the AFL-CIO.
Meany told him, "I can't help you now. But come back in ten years.
Most of you will have become employees. Then we will be able to
talk."

In retrospect, says Dr. Marcus, Meany's prediction was basically
accurate; he was wrong only about the time it would take. He decided to learn how to organize on his own. He took courses, starting
with labor law. And he turned to people with years of experience in
union organizing. He hired an experienced staff and let them do
what they were hired to do. He says, "I saw to it that good people
surrounded me. I always took all my employees from the labor movement. They were our mentors as well as our employees. Our attorneys were skilled in these things, in labor law. We never thought of
ourselves as high and mighty as most doctors do. We knew we had
to learn about this from experienced people."

Dr. Marcus began to travel around the country giving speeches
and listening to doctors tell him what they wanted. He recalls cover-
ing 50,000 miles in the first few years. "There were enough brush
fires across the country" that there was always some group interested

---

[1] The following is based on statements by Dr. Marcus, some of which are quoted directly and others paraphrased.

in hearing about physicians' unions. He says, "People become interested in joining unions because they are fed up. One joins out of hunger, not great philosophic reasoning."

The UAPD's First Year

The UAPD's identity and structure were largely forged during its first year, 1973. One early formative decision was whether to affiliate with the AFL-CIO. The choice had to be made because the UAPD had become involved in forming a federation of physicians' unions. On January, 16, the core membership of the UAPD met and agreed to join the American Federation of Physicians and Dentists as one of its founding chapters, but not to affiliate with the AFL-CIO. They agreed that George Meany's response to their initial request for support meant that they would receive little assistance from organized labor so there was no reason to affiliate.[2]

The Federation held its first meeting in February and elected officers. Stanley Peterson, M.D., of Springfield, Missouri was elected president; Donald Meyer, a dentist, became vice president, and Dr. Marcus was elected secretary (*UAPD Newsletter*, February 1973).[3]

[2] The union continued to explore affiliation with the AFL-CIO over the years. The August 1988 *UAPD Newsletter* made the observation that an AMA newsletter article stated that the AFL-CIO resolution recognizing the right of physicians to organize could turn AFL-CIO unions into allies and friends. It appears that the shift in the AFL-CIO's position toward doctors did encourage the UAPD to enter into discussions with organized labor to explore the possibility of affiliation the following year (*UAPD Newsletter*, May 1989). There has been no agreement to date.

[3] *UAPD Newsletter* refers to the publications issued by the union over the course of its history even though the newsletter went through numerous name changes. In 1972, it was called *Union of American Physicians News*; in 1975, it became *Union of American Physicians and Dentists News*. In 1978, it was the *Leadership News*. In 1981, it was renamed *UAPD National Report*. In 1982 it became the *UAPD Report*, and it continues to be published under that name. In 1981, the year that the state granted collective bargaining rights to employed physicians, the union created the California State Employed Physicians Association (SEPA) in order to give the salaried portion of the membership a separate identity, and began issuing a new publication, the *SEPA Newsletter*. *UAPD the Salaried Doctor* followed. All the newsletters are identified by month and year; some of the earlier issues also indicate a day of the month. With one exception, local branches of the union do not publish regular newsletters. The San Jose branch, headed by Dr. Weinmann until he became president of the union, operated as a local with its own newsletter called the *Bulletin of UAPD Local*

Some of the representatives from other states urged the Federation to affiliate with Big Labor. Others, including Dr. Marcus, were opposed. The Federation leadership ended up not taking a stance on affiliation, thus allowing chapters to make the decision for themselves.

From its earliest beginnings, the UAPD tried to appeal to two separate constituencies. Salaried physicians employed by the state of California were one audience; the other was physicians in private practice. Work had to proceed on separate fronts because the two categories had, and continue to have, very different concerns. The union has consistently attempted to give equal attention to both.

The UAPD began its official activities in January 1973 by renting office space and hiring a secretary (UAPD Newsletter, January 1973). In February, Dr. Marcus and a few close associates began meeting to discuss organizing activities. One of their first decisions was to develop a "system of shop stewards" with one steward per hospital (UAPD Newsletter, February 1973).

During its first half year the UAPD grew steadily. As a result, it could take on more staff and launch new activities by the month. In March, the union hired its first employee, to assist private practice physicians in their dealings with Blue Cross/Blue Shield. This turned out to be a pivotal move. The advisor was a highly experienced former BC/BS employee. She informed doctors through the newsletter that it was illegal for BC/BS to change the procedure number assigned by the physician in order to reimburse at a lower rate. She told them that patients could be reimbursed directly if they requested a special form; and explained what doctors should tell their patients to do to obtain reimbursement (UAPD Newsletter, March 1973). She made clear that she was there to help physicians recoup payments that somehow got fouled up in the BC/BS bureaucracy. She had work to do as soon as she came on board. The April newsletter announced a new full-time "coordinator of union organization." This is the position Gary Robinson, now the executive director, assumed initially; as the organization grew, the position evolved into the directorship.

7402, which I cite in Chapter 14. The president periodically sent letters to the entire membership to draw attention to particularly noteworthy events. I refer to all the newsletters issued from the union's headquarters as the UAPD Newsletter.

The newsletter reported during the union's first year that Dr. Marcus met several times with the AMA leadership to ask its support for physicians' unionizing efforts. The AMA repeatedly declined. In fact, the AMA issued a policy statement that year stating that it was unalterably opposed to physicians unions but that doctors were, of course, free to join unions as individuals.

Dr. Marcus sought the advice of Dr. Hugh Faulkner, head of the British Practitioners' Union, in the summer of 1973. The union was generous with moral support and advice for the fledgling California group. Dr. Marcus kept in contact with both the Practitioners' Union and the British Medical Association. He visited the BMA in 1981 to learn negotiating tactics (*UAPD Newsletter*, May 1981).

By August, it became necessary to hire another full-time clerical employee and a new part-timer in October. The "Insurance Grievance Department" was the new label assigned to the job of assisting doctors in private practice to collect fees from third-party payers. The grievance department was clearly beginning to achieve impressive results. In one case, a physician hand-carried many months' worth of claims to BC/BS on the day they were due, only to see them rejected for lateness. With the assistance of the grievance department, he was issued a check for $4,044. Three similar cases followed within the month. By the end of the year, the Insurance Grievance Department had developed a "disputed claim form" that simplified the process of filing such claims, available to members without charge. By the middle of the following year, the department reported that it had recovered nearly a million dollars.

By the end of 1973, the UAPD looked very much like a going concern. The union now had two people engaged full-time in union organizing and three clerical workers. For his part, Dr. Marcus was devoting an ever-increasing number of hours to union activities— being interviewed, speaking to groups across the country, running the UAPD, plus playing an active role in the national Federation.

The union was also making early gains in its efforts to organize salaried physicians. Although it would take another decade to establish fully functioning collective bargaining units, the city of San Francisco enacted an ordinance giving the UAPD the right to form a bargaining unit exclusively representing salaried physicians and dentists. This permitted the UAPD to act as the doctors' representative in discussions with the city. However, the union could not bargain over salaries until the state passed legislation to permit this in 1981.[4]

The city's decision to permit the UAPD to represent employed physicians and dentists was immediately opposed by the American Federation of State, County and Municipal Employees (AFSCME), which sued to overturn the decision. The UAPD's response was that AFSCME was insisting on keeping salaried physicians "in an illegal bargaining unit consisting of kitchen helpers, custodial employees and other non-professionals." In effect, AFSCME did not want physicians to organize into their own bargaining units separate from other hospital employees. Of the 1,000 doctors employed by the state who were eligible to vote in a secret ballot election, 437 voted for the UAPD and 137 for the AFSCME sponsored union (*UAPD Newsletter*, August 1981:1).

While the UAPD could not officially serve as a collective bargaining agent for the salaried doctors and dentists who became members, it could and did mediate disputes even where it was not the recognized representative. The October 1974 newsletter reported that UAPD prevented the dismissal of physicians at San Francisco General Hospital who were attached to the Psychiatric Emergency Service. The union received much positive attention for its role in helping to avert a crisis, in a front-page story in the *San Francisco Examiner* (September 4, 1974).

The Malpractice Crisis Years

In 1975 the malpractice crisis took center stage in the union's activities. When the malpractice insurance rate went up by 486%, San Francisco anesthesiologists simply walked out for four weeks—the first phase of the strike discussed in Chapter 3. The UAPD helped to reach a settlement. While the union leadership was responsive to the membership's commitment to a statewide job action on the date the malpractice premiums were scheduled to take effect, it worked to find a more permanent resolution to the crisis. Leaders'

---

[4] California's Supreme Court approved collective bargaining for physicians employed by the state in a 4-2 decision in 1981 ("Collective Bargaining . . . ," 1981).

efforts satisfied members and impressed various interested parties watching from the sidelines. The UAPD's highly visible public profile undoubtedly was responsible for bringing in new members during this period.

In addition to the efforts the union was devoting to the strike, the malpractice crisis was creating ripple effects that required much of the staff's time and energy. For example, the UAPD became enmeshed in a battle when a San Francisco hospital fired fourteen physicians who refused to carry malpractice insurance. The union took the position that the hospital was infringing on the physicians' right to make their own decisions about assuming the risks involved. The hospitals were destined to win this battle over time. They could simply refuse to appoint new doctors to the staff if they did not carry malpractice insurance. In recollecting this period, Dr. Marcus says that he realized the union would have to give up this fight, but that the whole malpractice issue was such a sore point that it was contributing to ill will all around.

That the malpractice issue was having a wearing effect on everyone involved is illustrated by an item in the October 1975 newsletter. The story indicates that doctors were becoming increasingly short-tempered and distrustful of all the organizations with which they were associated, even the union. Some members decided to challenge the steady rise in dues, which had climbed to $161 per year. The treasurer responded in the newsletter by reporting that the UAPD was spending $95 on services delivered from headquarters, $36 was remitted to the national Federation, and the remainder went for specific objectives in various locations, including organizing.

The union's membership had grown steadily during the first few years. Dr. Marcus's efforts to reach a wider audience by putting his ideas into print were clearly producing results. He attracted the interest of physicians who previously would not have considered unionization through an essay in a March 1975 issue of *Medical Economics*. Dr. Marcus wrote that he was responding to California Congressman Ronald Dellums's proposal that doctors should be paid a salary of $30,000 to $50,000 per year. He noted that, as a result of negotiations, the 1975 salary for municipal laborers in San Francisco would be $19,075 and $25,250 for the city's truck drivers. This was the same week that senior pilots at Delta had signed a new contract

with a salary of $100,000 per year. Dr. Marcus's point was that join-
ing a union is a prerequisite to bargaining for higher pay. In answer
to the obvious question, bargaining with whom? He answered: ". . .
[W]e're rapidly progressing toward the day when the Government
will become the sole purchaser of health care . . . and thus our only
paymaster. The free market will vanish" (1975a: 205).

He went on to compare the difficulty of pilots' work and doctors'
work, extracting excellent bargaining points from the comparison.
In fact, he concluded that doctors would benefit by using the pilots'
union as a model. However, he feared that physicians were not ready
to come together. The major obstacle was the disparity in medical
incomes: "There's no justification for the services of one doctor com-
manding an income 20 times that of an equally conscientious practitioner" (1975a:211). He proposed the following solution: "Our first
step should be to set up a relative-value scale. . . . The ultimate
purpose would be to make sure that the surgeon who does one open-
heart operation a month won't command 10 times the income of the
pediatrician who works 70 hours a week" (1975a:211–212).[5]

As a surgeon, Dr. Marcus felt he was in a good position to make
observations about the incomes of fellow surgeons. He noted that
surgeons were members of specialties considered the most glamorous
and highest paid. He warned them, however, that the influx of new
recruits was "turning glamour into glut." He concluded:

> . . . Doctors must change their whole perspective and thinking
> about the economic future of medicine. They've been so preoc-
> cupied with fees under possible Government domination that
> they've lost sight of the larger issues—total compensation and
> relative economic worth. . . . After all, no one wants to fly with
> an airline pilot who's disgruntled because he isn't getting paid
> enough. Similarly, we can demonstrate that a fair compensation
> for doctor's services will help to increase the chances of high-
> quality patient care. (1975a:214)

[5] The Health Care Financing Administration, the agency responsible for administering
Medicare, has adopted a version of this reimbursement plan. The Resource Based Relative
Value Scale (RBRVS) was the result of extensive research, planning, and negotiation ef-
forts headed by Hsiao (1988).

Over the next few years, Dr. Marcus repeatedly invoked the comparison between doctors and pilots to illustrate the benefits of unionization. For example, in a 1981 letter to members, he pointed out that annual UAPD dues were very low at $280, compared to the pilots' dues of 1.36 percent of annual income. He argued that the pilots' high dues were instrumental in achieving remarkable gains—an 18-hour work week, retirement at 59, and annual salaries of $130,000. The contrast with the work situation of salaried physicians was apparently obvious.

It is impossible to determine whether the UAPD's early membership growth was due to word of mouth, the effectiveness of the union's organizers, or Dr. Marcus's tireless efforts and skills. However, Gary Robinson says that Dr. Marcus's presentations never failed to bring in new members. He recalled an early speaking engagement, in a hospital conference room on a rainy evening in New York City. About 50 physicians were there. It was around 8 o'clock in the evening; they were tired; they were dragging themselves in. Dr. Marcus began by telling them that they had had it soft on their pedestals. That got their attention. As Robinson puts it, Dr. Marcus said a lot of things these guys would not have accepted from anyone else. He always talked off the cuff, with no notes. By the time he had finished, the doctors were standing on their chairs, yelling and cheering. Robinson said it was an amazing thing to watch, and Dr. Marcus did it every time. In this case, the audience included physicians ranging widely in age, specialty, and ethnicity. Yet, Robinson says, it was clear that each member of that audience heard what he or she wanted to hear and was energized by it.

By the end of 1975, Dr. Marcus had begun to feel the economic consequences of the time he was spending on union activities. The executive board decided he should be compensated for "release time" spent on union activities, and he became a paid officer of the union.

While the malpractice crisis may have had the effect of galvanizing doctors across the country while it lasted, it did not benefit the physicians' union movement. The movement's record of gains and losses at the national level was uneven during the middle years of the decade. The Federation of American Physicians and Dentists had begun to fall apart. In fact, the UAPD allowed its affiliation with the Federation to lapse in 1974 because it was so disorganized. At the same time, physicians across the country were banding together to establish new local unions.

When the union movement at the national level was left with neither a platform nor a recognized spokesman, grass-roots organizers in other states began asking to affiliate with the UAPD directly. By late 1975, the UAPD was entertaining expressions of interest from the Arizona Professional Guild, the Oregon Federation of Physicians, and a group in the process of becoming established in Iowa. The UAPD agreed to accept the emergent unions as affiliates before determining the privileges and responsibilities this would entail. The executive director, Gary Robinson, says that the union learned its lesson during this period. The affiliates faded out of existence because they did not take direction from the UAPD headquarters. Robinson says that the new physicians' unions emerging along the west coast asking to affiliate in the 1990s will be allowed to affiliate only if they agree to have staff persons from the union's headquarters involved.

A Failed Union

The UAPD grew and established itself as an organization while most other physicians' unions were floundering and failing. Most impressive was Dr. Marcus's success in making the transition from social movement to a more stable form of organization. He was responsible for organizing the initial protest group and giving it a union identity. It was basically his decision first to participate in the larger physicians' union movement and later to withdraw from it. He continued to identify the services the union would institute and develop. In essence, he was responsible for shaping the structure that permitted the UAPD to evolve into a firmly established organization.

Why did other doctors' unions fail? While it may not be possible to generalize from the experience of the Illinois Physicians Union (IPU), its demise provides some insight. The IPU charter was signed by the fifteen persons who attended the first meeting. I interviewed ten of these founding members. All said they attended the first meeting in the expectation of seeing a vigorous new physicians' organization established as an alternative to the AMA. This, however, was where the consensus about the group's function fell apart. The participants quickly determined that their views could not be reconciled.

A young general surgeon explained why he wanted to join an activist group and why he became "disenchanted" once he saw who else was there:

> The AMA is too conservative. I was interested in participating in a strong political body to change the image of doctors. I am interested in strong policing, peer review. I have no compunctions about reporting wrongdoings. I have no delusions that there are some physicians who are not competent.
> . . . We were supposed to be an activist group. Let's try to be active, fight hospitals that are making practice difficult. The hospital I was in, where there were two or three administrators, after five years, there are now two or three dozen administrators generating costs, legislating what we can do. . . . I felt the people at the meeting were fighting for things I am against. They're fighting to have G.P.'s do surgery.

Another founding member came to the meeting with a more philosophical perspective. As a psychiatrist who had recently accepted a half-time administrative position in a community hospital, his interest in supporting a physicians' union was that it would "make a statement." At the same time, he held out little hope that it would achieve any specific objectives.

> I thought if physicians unionized they would be able to articulate their needs. The decision to join was the quantum leap to see themselves as a body of people practicing self-interest in a conflictual situation. It wasn't the union activities that I thought would be so particularly useful, but the decision to unionize. It was a failure. People didn't join. . . . They couldn't bring themselves to see that a new age was dawning. . . . The physicians are being coopted. They're stupid. Administration says we've got a lot in common; let's work together. They think they'll get the breaks. This is self-delusion.

Asked why he didn't stay active in the union the psychiatrist said, "I was a bum. It was a financial drain. I left because nothing was hap-

pening. . . . I had a high-falutin' hypothetical reason for joining. . . .
If the AMA needed to go into the popcorn business to exist, it would
go into the popcorn business. American institutions are flexible."

In short, although the initial meeting attracted doctors who were
prepared to join as radical an organization as a physicians' union,
they could not overcome their differences over the problems they
expected the union to address. They were not willing to attend a
second meeting. In fact, the IPU never had regularly scheduled
meetings. Founder Dr. George Lagorio met with individuals and
small groups of physicians on an ad hoc basis, when they wanted to
hear his views on taking action on their own specific problems.
These doctors were generally not members of the IPU.

The IPU persisted for five or six years, operating on this basis.
Doctors continued to seek out the union for instrumental reasons,
because the IPU, in the person of Dr. Lagorio, agreed to help them
when no one else would. They joined the union at a point of crisis.
Once the crisis passed, they lost interest in the union. Because the
IPU could not develop a stable dues-paying membership, it could
not afford to hire staff. Dr. Lagorio was the organization. The IPU
persisted as long as he had the will to keep it going.

The IPU survived as long as the larger physicians' union movement gave it momentum. This is in contrast to the UAPD, which
succeeded by identifying services that large numbers of doctors
found beneficial and by developing the structure to deliver such services, along with collecting dues and reporting achievements—in
short, building a stable organization.

Even though the UAPD was well established by the close of the
1970s, Dr. Marcus was not in a position to rest on his laurels. As we
shall see in the following chapters, the process of institution-building
did not end, because the environment in which the UAPD was born
was short-lived. The health sector was about to undergo extensive
change during the 1980s that would take the UAPD in a different
direction. Chapter 7 focuses on these changes.

❧ 7 ❧

The Changing Environment
in the 1980s

The health care sector underwent significant alterations in the late 1970s and the 1980s, including the closure of many small and medium-size hospitals, mergers and buy-outs, and management contracts that brought together non-profit hospitals and for-profit management firms. In retrospect we can see that the aspirations for improving society that characterized the 1960s created unreasonable expectations of the speed at which change would occur. This vigorous agenda for changing health care delivery arrangements left little time to evaluate the implications of the structural changes that were already in process. In the short run, society did develop explanations for the trends that had begun to emerge at the time. The absence of dramatic improvements either in people's health or in the responsiveness of health organizations to the public's expectations required an explanation. The interpretation that had greatest appeal laid the blame on doctors and fostered a steady stream of anti-physician rhetoric.

From Regulation to Competition

The enthusiasm that greeted the Reagan presidential campaign signaled a major shift in the way society proposed to address its problems. This shift is reflected in the policy changes implemented during the 1980s.[1] The primary problem facing the health care sys-

[1] Given the popularity of the market approach during the 1980s, it is interesting to note the inconsistency between the government's rhetoric and its programs. It was during the early 1980s that the government calculated a set of prices it would pay to hospitals for particular episodes of hospitalization for patients on Medicare, on the basis of Diagnostic

tem was no longer defined as inadequate access but as a pressing need to contain costs. The framework of regulatory mechanisms was swept away and replaced by policies designed to support market mechanisms which, the new generation of policy makers promised, would achieve two desirable objectives—cost control and consumer choice of services.

Advocates of market solutions predicted that competition would make health care organizations more responsive to patient preferences for convenience and other amenities; produce more specialized services, for such segments as women, those with sports injuries, and those wanting to end addictive behaviors; identify and respond to a range of unmet patient demands; and result in greater differentiation of products and services from which patients could choose (Ginzberg, 1982; Feldstein, 1981; Greenberg, 1978). They argued that once the supply of physicians was large enough, it would match demand for health care services, and prices would ultimately fall.

The new generation of policy makers determined that only one of the many initiatives advocated by their predecessors should be given full support. Increased health manpower—meant to improve access during the 1960s and 1970s—would now solve a very different problem. The policy makers of the 1980s would increase the supply of health manpower in order to cut costs.

Not everyone expected increasing the supply of physicians to be socially beneficial. By the mid-1970s, some in the medical community had begun to warn of a physician surplus. By the end of the decade the federal government took notice and established a committee to project manpower requirements. The Graduate Medical Education National Advisory Committee (GMENAC), established in 1977, determined that there were sufficient numbers of physicians in

---

Related Group designations or DRGs (Budrys, 1986). This regulatory program turned out to be far more controlling than any other the government had legislated to date. How this could have occurred without much opposition from market proponents is not clear. The planning that went into designing the DRG program was very public, involving much negotiation with providers. In fact, various observers pointed out that providers prepared for DRGs by adjusting their prices in advance. The process was repeated when the effort to create a Resource Based Relative Value Scale (RBRVS) for paying doctors for Medicare services was launched during the latter half of the 1980s. This reimbursement program went into effect in January 1992.

all but a few specialty areas, namely psychiatry, emergency medicine, nuclear medicine, and, to a lesser extent, some branches of pediatrics, preventive medicine, and anesthesiology. More importantly, the committee concluded that there was an impending serious oversupply of surgeons. The Reagan administration allowed the GMENAC report to languish.[2]

Interpreting the Legacy of Competition

The most significant change in the health care system during the latter half of the 1970s was the entry of for-profit organizations. Advocates of the market approach and the benefits of competition had not received nearly as much public support in the past. The election of Ronald Reagan signaled the shift in the public's attitude in favor of market mechanisms in health care. The medical community was pleased with the shift away from control imposed by the government and looked forward to market controls as liberating.

Not everyone in the medical community welcomed market forces, however. For one, Arnold Relman, the highly respected editor of the *New England Journal of Medicine*, proclaimed in a 1980 editorial that, in economic potential, the health care sector was replacing the military sector. The growing interdependence of medicine and industry, Relman warned, had spawned a dangerous alliance—a medical-industrial complex. Doctors were becoming excessively entrepreneurial and at risk of losing their professional, humanitarian ideals. He argued that physicians would lose their ability to influence the functioning of the health care system because other, more powerful, forces would control its future. Health care organizations now risked being driven by the need to improve economic productivity rather than the need to improve health. He predicted that the emergent medical-industrial complex would take on a life of its own. His warnings were considered extreme at the time. They are now regarded as truly prescient and are repeatedly cited.

[2] The states with the highest ratio of physicians to the population were the states in which the physicians' union movement emerged. Four of the states which have had the highest rate of growth or consistently exhibited the highest ratios in the country are New York, Massachusetts, California, and Florida (Owens, 1987).

Dr. Marcus outlined his attitude toward the growing power of the corporate sector in the *New England Journal of Medicine* in 1984:

> Because the personal doctor-patient relationship appeared to be most imperiled by the direct involvement of government in the financing and distribution of health care, the attention of most American doctors has been directed toward this "threat from the left"; this has distracted them from noticing that their profession was becoming at least as vulnerable to a corporate takeover by bigger and stronger members of the entrepreneurial class, with whom they had come to identify themselves so closely. . . . The ultimate consideration that now makes the position of doctors so untenable is the commitment of government at all levels to the so-called "pro-competition" system of health-care delivery through the enactment of legislation that places all the trump cards in the hands of these paymasters. (1984a:1508)

When some health care costs did begin to show signs of slowing down in the early 1980s, proponents of the market immediately took credit. The cost of hospitalization leveled off the most, and the length of hospital stays decreased. Proponents of market mechanisms attributed this trend to competition among hospitals. Another contingent credited the trend to increasing HMO enrollments; HMOs, they said, were holding down their rates to achieve a competitive edge. Some observers argued that the decline in length of hospital stays was due to the DRG; they attributed the slow-down in hospital cost increases to a leveling off of the elevated charges put in effect in anticipation of the DRGs. The matter was largely settled when Sloan and Valvona convincingly argued that advances in medical technology and surgical technique had done the most to reduce hospital stays (1986).

Belief in the ability of HMOs to contain health care costs has nevertheless continued. Comparisons have consistently been made between regions with high and low HMO enrollments (Luft, 1987). The Twin Cities have long had the highest HMO market penetration of any area in the country. As a result some have seen trends in this area as indicators of things to come across the country. Initially attention was focused on the reactions of patients, i.e., their satisfaction, enrollment rates, disenrollments, and hospitalization rates. More recently, interest has been turning toward the steps taken by physicians in response to declining starting salaries and increasing pressure to reduce costs (Meyer, 1987).

By the late 1980s, competition in the Twin Cities had become intense, with 95 percent of the physicians contracting with one of the HMOs in the area. The Physicians Health Plan of Minneapolis/ St. Paul, which was one of the largest HMOs in the country during the late 1980s, made an unprecedented move. It announced it would withhold 20 to 30 percent of doctors' reimbursements in a contingency fund and, furthermore, that it planned to introduce more permanent pay cuts. The physicians filed a lawsuit charging mismanagement and conflicts of interest. The HMO countersued. Spokesmen for the physicians who instituted the suit said that a new group numbering 1,000 physicians had begun discussing the possibility of forming a union. When a reporter asked why, one doctor said that only a few years ago he would have thought unionization unprofessional, but physicians were losing too much control and drastic steps were indicated (Johnson, 1987).

Paul Ellwood, long recognized as the single most adamant advocate of HMOs, said that this doctors' rebellion marked a "critical turning point." "There are few places where it's gone as far as it has here," Ellwood noted, "but it's moving in that direction everywhere" (Johnson, 1987). Comments such as those by Dr. Richard Reese, a health care consultant, must have alerted Ellwood to the depth of feeling among physicians: "Paul Ellwood . . . keeps making these prophecies that we're going to have eight to 10 'supermeds' running the system; I'm making a prophecy that we're going to have an organized opposition to this corporate takeover. I'm saying the game isn't over yet. You're seeing these forces start to emerge in mature markets" (Scheier, 1986:reprint, no page).

The changes of the late 1970s and 1980s had the effect of creating health care organizations that were larger, more centralized, and in a better position to impose controls over medical work. This, in turn, raised questions about medical professionalism which continue to be debated. Before examining the steps the UAPD took in response to the changes in its environment, let us examine the meaning and value of professionalism in the larger context.

❧ 8 ❧

The Deprofessionalization
of Medicine?

The institutional changes of the 1970s and 1980s were often justified by the need to control the excesses of "providers," the new label for doctors and administrators of health care institutions. Public attitude surveys indicated support for this perspective. They also revealed some interesting inconsistencies.

Blendon and Altman described the public's attitude as schizophrenic (1984). Survey respondents expressed a low level of confidence in the medical profession as a whole while registering a high degree of satisfaction and confidence in their own doctors.[1] Dr. Marcus saw dangers in this inconsistency:

> Periodic "fixes" we get from Gallup polls that tell us how loved we are, are addictive illusions. Polls are always worded to direct attention to "my doctor," with whom most respondents have enjoyed a good and strong relationship—until now, that is.
>
> But when the medical profession as a class is the object of the inquiry, terms such as "too rich," "uncaring," "haughty," "unavailable," or "interested only in money" surface quickly. This naive failure to recognize that the medical profession is simply a composite of "my doctors" is the product of what seems to be a carefully orchestrated program of denigration by

[1] One possible interpretation of this finding is that patients are willing to invest a great deal of trust in, even dependency on, their own physicians because they see direct benefits from the investment they make in maintaining a satisfying doctor/patient relationship (Budrys, 1993). This is in contrast to the public's perception of the value of investing trust in medicine as an institution.

those who perceive us only as a means to a corporate end.
(1984b:42)

Dr. Marcus used the experience of teachers to illustrate the fate
that could befall medicine:

> The deliberate creation of a whipping-boy to divert attention
> from the real problems of society has ample precedent in the
> case of the teaching profession, where teachers have been un-
> fairly saddled with the consequences of the breakup of the
> American family, together with the resulting problems in disci-
> pline and learning. They have also been handed the task of
> integrating society harmoniously, all the while being expected
> to keep the United States in the forefront of the world in scien-
> tific and mathematical knowledge and in general literacy.
>
> Their inability to accomplish these impossible tasks single-
> handedly, together with the attendant blame that has been
> heaped upon them for not doing so, have had tragic conse-
> quences. Not only is public education in the United States in
> total disarray with embarrassingly low standards everywhere,
> but—and most ominously—the teaching profession has be-
> come demoralized. . . .
>
> As a final bit of irony, a recent Rand Corporation report
> suggests we may have to offer tomorrow's teachers a salary of
> as much as $50,000 per year to attract the brightest and the
> best young people to that profession! The tragic lesson of hav-
> ing to reinvent the wheel by rebuilding the pride and motiva-
> tion of a profession that had already earned the esteem of soci-
> ety, should not be wasted by a reenactment of the same
> scenario with the medical profession. (1985:unpaginated re-
> print)

Dr. Marcus repeatedly warned doctors that their attitude permitted them to deny how much control they had lost. "'Professionalism,'" he wrote, "is a term that once connoted both expertise *and*
adherence to lofty principle. But can one still remain a professional,
while acquiescing in the denial of treatment by a medical ration
board, and at a time when the denied treatment is still being taught

in our research and training institutions as the best one available?"
(1989a:reprint, no page).

In the same essay, he argued that clinging to the language of
professionalism was standing in the way of progress: "A modern army
would not stand much chance of defending itself if it insisted on
each of its soldiers' wearing a full clanking suit of medieval armor.
Yet the medical profession is trying to fend off or at least soften its
own proletarianization, no less weighted down with concepts and
nomenclature that have become hopelessly outdated and inappropriate."

New Forms of Social Control vs. Professionalism

The institutional changes of the 1970s did not result in enough
change to satisfy society. The social consensus was that the regulatory approach had failed. However, the sense that greater social control over medical work was necessary did not abate (Roemer, 1986).
During the 1980s, policy makers argued that market-oriented techniques would give decision-making power back to the consumer.
Corporate executives responded by introducing an array of competitive approaches and well-established managerial techniques.

Doctors could not ignore the fact that references to their professionalism were no longer producing the same degree of social regard
and reward as in the past. They were uncertain, however, about what
had caused this to happen. I argue that society became less willing to
accept the value of professionalism because the crucial social control
function it has traditionally fulfilled could be, and increasingly was
being, addressed by other, more powerful mechanisms. In Chapter
4, I argued that professionalism evolved as the primary mechanism
of social control over medical work because bureaucratic measures
simply could not have been imposed on the structure of medical
practice at that time—solo, fee-for-service practices in widely scattered private offices. The arrangement that evolved, grounded in
professionalism, meant that society extended to medicine a social
mandate, in recognition of the profession's commitment to maintain
strict controls over its members. It was expected to do so, first,
through an extended period of education and socialization and, second, by taking responsibility for improving the quality of medical

care and for identifying incompetent doctors and preventing them from harming patients. The agreement required a considerable degree of public trust, which the profession succeeded in garnering.

In Chapter 7, I noted that one of the arguments for introducing market mechanisms during the 1980s was the claim that the professional dominance of doctors permitted them to ignore market controls; this dominance was targeted as a major reason for rising costs. Accordingly, policy makers passed laws aimed at imposing greater control over doctors' treatment decisions and the charges accompanying those decisions. By the end of the decade, the degree of oversight was, according to Bradford Gray, unparalleled elsewhere in society (1991:243).[2]

As discussed in Chapter 5, a variety of forces led to the decline of professionalism as the primary control over physicians' work. These included the distrust of social institutions that emerged during the 1960s, the feminist critique of medicine, and the emergence of constituencies with their own demands, for example, the disabled, mentally ill, and aged. In addition, the profession was undergoing internal structural changes—the growth of group practice and extensive subspecialization, for example. Finally, hospitals were imposing stricter controls over the range of procedures a physician could perform.

Together, these changes have had the effect of causing patients to see a greater number of doctors who, in turn, are in a position to review and comment on the treatments prescribed by their colleagues. As a consequence, deviant practices and incompetence are now much more likely to be identified and controlled. The consumers of medical care, that is, patients, seem to believe they now have more protection, even if, from their perspective, control is imposed only because the organizations involved are self-interested and eager to prevent actions that might result in a lawsuit. A new occupation, risk management, has come into existence during this period. Risk managers must identify and correct risky situations, and, perhaps even more important, convince consumers that their interests are being protected (Leyerle, 1984, 1994).

[2] Ritzer and Walczak identify this as the "spread of formal rationality," which they link to deprofessionalization (1988).

Curiously, the single most powerful control mechanism to emerge during this period has attracted very little scrutiny from either practitioners or scholars (Borzo, 1993, 1994).[3] This mechanism is the computerized patient file, which was not intentionally designed to have any consequences for medical professionalism. Questions about how the files might be used are only beginning to be formulated, and perhaps because they are not seen as a particularly radical departure from earlier record-keeping practices. Doctors seem to lump together the requirement that records be entered into computerized systems with the whole range of control mechanisms, that is, the "hassle factor" (Epstein, 1993). Since computerization is occurring across all sectors of society, it is not perceived as specifically threatening to doctors. It is, however, becoming increasingly clear that patient files can be used as highly efficient work-monitoring devices.

Computerized record-keeping was given considerable impetus by third-party payers who would reimburse only with evidence of treatment. Once a detailed and easily accessed patient file existed, it was logical to use the file as evidence of treatment procedures as well. The fact that the record permitted profiling of treatment patterns, evaluation of quality, and computation of the resources the physician used per case was not initially a concern. Rather than resolving the problem of monitoring doctors' work more effectively, computerization creates a new social problem. The availability of a highly effective instrument of control is shifting the question from *how* to impose control to *who* will control.

According to John Meyer (1986), professionalism has been the preferred American response to situations of technological uncertainty. But the current sense of unease about computers is producing the opposite response—less reliance on doctors' claims to professionalism. Most people are not qualified to judge whether the sophisticated new technology is, in fact, more efficacious. Those who capture control of the mechanisms that analyze the relationship between treatments and outcomes will be in the best position to define the rules regarding treatment protocols. They will also be in

---

[3] This is not because medicine has been totally unprepared for the impact of computer applications. Discussion of clinical applications and their implications began to appear in the medical press by the early 1970s (Schwartz, 1970; McKinlay, 1973).

an excellent position to influence public attitudes about value of medical professionalism as opposed to other, more "rational" forms of control.

Corporate executives of health sector organizations who claim that more "rational" controls must be imposed on the medical profession have been actively creating institutional mechanisms to do so. They have a vested interest in maintaining such arrangements. In order to guarantee survival of the entities they have created, they must convince the public that these mechanisms are succeeding in imposing socially beneficial controls over medical work. And society must concur in, or at least not reject, this definition of the situation. In short, society must accept the definition offered by corporations: that corporate managerial tools will result in better control over the work doctors do than will collegiality and professionalism.

Paul Starr was one of the first to point out, as early as 1982, that self-interested corporations pose a greater threat than self-interested doctors. Starr questioned medicine's claims to altruism, but he made clear that control based on professionalism is far better for society than control by market-oriented organizations. He noted that the medical profession includes many independent-minded individuals who do not always agree on matters of professional interest, many of whom are truly dedicated to improving patients' health rather than adding to their bank accounts. By contrast, the corporation is a highly centralized, far more single-minded entity dedicated, first and foremost, to the pursuit of profit.

Is Professionalism on the Decline?

As health care organizations grow larger, more centralized and hierarchically controlled, and more overtly committed to market forces, doctors find that they cannot ignore the rules and requirements the corporate decision-makers are imposing. Much of the growth is the result of mergers, acquisitions, and joint ventures involving hospitals, managed care organizations, and doctors' practice groups which may, in turn, be networked via ties to insurance companies. It is often difficult to know what the linkages are, when they were established, and if or how they change. Social scientists and others interested in medicine's fate have been watching and debating the effect of such trends on medical work (Gray, 1991; Light, 1986; Ginzberg, 1990, 1985). Concern about the extent to which the growth of the corporate sector will erode medical professionalism and whether this will hurt the quality of care is fostering a renewed interest in professionalism. The basic question is whether medical professionalism is, in fact, declining (Hafferty and McKinlay, 1993; Light and Levine, 1988; Richmond and Fein, 1995; Wolinsky, 1993, 1988).

Some observers have argued that medicine has been declining in status and symbolic rewards since the late 1960s, that it is becoming "deprofessionalized." Marie Haug, for example, has argued that patients are becoming far better informed and therefore more assertive about assessing the need for treatments (1973, 1988). She predicted that computers would play a crucial role in disseminating knowledge, and sees patient power as going hand in hand with deprofessionalization of doctors' role. It is clear that computers are producing a great deal of information about medical practice, but it is not at all clear that individual patients are benefiting. The corporate sector is using computers to assess the costs and benefits of various treatment options. If medicine is more carefully monitored by corporations and the third-party payers with which corporations contract to provide care for their employees, do patients necessarily benefit?

The argument that computerization leads to deprofessionalization does not take into account the fact that medical science has been producing knowledge at a faster pace than computers can translate it into information that might be useful to patients. Clinicians simply cannot translate scientific breakthroughs into medical applications at the same pace that science can reveal potential new applications. Clinical trials to determine the efficacy and side effects of experimental applications require even more time. It is hard to understand how patients could make informed judgments if the experts themselves are not sure about risks and expected treatment outcomes.

Haug agrees that it is difficult to know whether medicine is becoming deprofessionalized more quickly now (1994). The lack of evidence has prompted some observers to suggest that the deprofessionalization perspective may be grounded in the "politics of envy" (Starr, 1982). The "wishful thinking" interpretation suggests that social scientists may be unconsciously hoping that a drop in doctors' status may lead to a proportional increase in their own status and income (Evans, 1986). Others have argued that, rather than being deprofessionalized, medicine is being proletarianized (McKinlay and Arches, 1985). This argument grows out of a different perspective from the deprofessionalization perspective. I take up the proletarianization argument in Chapter 11, in the context of a larger discussion of the changing structure of work.

How independent must practice be to be professional? Is medical professionalism threatened when doctors affiliate with large organizations? Earlier discussions did not differentiate between not-for-profit organizations and for-profit organizations because the number of for-profit organizations in the health sector was so small. More recently, such discussions have been primarily focused on the threat that stems from "corporatization" or corporate take-over of health care (Stoeckle, 1988).

The idea that accepting a salaried position *per se* has deprofessionalizing effects seems to be a concern that is peculiar to Americans. According to Larson, however (whose analysis predates the current concern about the implications of corporatization) it is a preoccupation in English-speaking countries (1977). Larson notes that European physicians who work for a salary are recognized as high-status professionals. Ironically, in Great Britain the higher-status specialists are salaried while the general practitioners are paid by capitation.

The characteristics American doctors chose to embrace in constructing a definition of professionalism—independently organized private practices and fee-for-service reimbursement arrangements—are so deeply ingrained and linked to the idealized self-image doctors wanted to project that medicine is now having a difficult time coping with a changing occupational reality. The lack of alternative culturally acceptable models makes the process of adjusting even more difficult. It may be accurate to say that, until relatively recently, in the midst of a capitalist society the medical profession has operated as a precapitalist guild (Light and Levine, 1988). But is it accurate to treat the collapse of this arrangement as evidence of declining professionalism? I return to this topic in Chapters 11 and 12.

Talk about deprofessionalization and other indicators of their declining collective power and individual autonomy has exacerbated the sense of threat that physicians are now experiencing. Spokesmen with very different views of what a better health care system means, for example, James Sammons then the executive vice-president of the AMA (Sammons, 1976) and Paul Ellwood, the leading proponent of managed care (Johnson, 1987)—have said that the emergence of physicians' unions signals the decline of doctors' social status. Both argue that physician unionism should be viewed as the first step in sure descent from middle class to working class status. Physicians are susceptible to this imagery because they are already experiencing the negative impact of bureaucratization on their work lives. There is no question that their work autonomy is being restricted. That they fear even greater loss of autonomy to unions is understandable. The identity long associated with American unions, which is grounded in industrial unionism—organizing by firm, calling for working class solidarity, and restricting individual opportunity in preference for collective security—clearly holds no appeal for physicians.

The UAPD's success in overcoming the powerful negative imagery associated with unions is therefore all the more remarkable. Its ability to survive and flourish over the course of tumultuous change in the health care sector merits even more recognition. It indicates that the UAPD leadership was able, first, to identify the factors responsible for the work frustrations doctors were confronting even as the factors themselves were shifting and, second, to develop mechanisms to address them. Let us now turn to the UAPD's operations during its second decade.

❧ 9 ☙

The Mature Organization

According to Dr. Marcus, the UAPD helped more and more physicians who were being treated unfairly during the 1980s. He argued that doctor-bashing, which had reached unprecedented heights, was at least partially responsible. The most prominent aggressors were the media and the corporate interests whose views the media were reporting.[1] In response to the notion that doctors were unavailable, uncaring, and interested only in money, he wrote:

> This is the new litany of the talk shows and the checkout stand tabloids, that is now appearing with increasing frequency in the more responsible segments of the press and proper drawing rooms in the country. From a quasi-priesthood that once represented the apex of every doting parent's ambitions for his or her child, the medical profession is privately anguishing over its rapid fall from the esteem it once held. . . . However, there is a growing feeling among many doctors, that this present frenzy of doctor-bashing is not just a spontaneous manifestation of fair criticism but rather that it represents a carefully-orchestrated scenario designed to reduce society's esteem for what has been a basically decent and hard-working group of professionals.
>
> To give the devil his due, the medical profession has certainly been guilty of not trying hard enough to dispel the romanticized notions of its own infallibility. (1985:unpaginated reprint)

The doctor bashers argued that the corporate sector would curb doctors' reliance on the most costly but not necessarily most effec-

---

[1] For graphic confirmation of this assessment see Leyerle (1994, 1984).

tive treatments. Dr. Marcus labeled the corporations who were becoming so prevalent the "new paymasters," noting that they were
now in the position to present doctors with take-it-or-leave-it offers.
He followed with his standing argument—that the only way to
counter this situation was to organize collectively: "With the cash
flow of the health-care industry now coming under almost total control of a new class of managers, a trade union offers the only vehicle
that doctors, as de facto employees of those managers, can use to
develop effective negotiating power given the new market conditions under which they must now serve" (1984a:1509).

Dr. Marcus makes the same point in the journal *Private Practice* in
1984, but adds a few more colorful quips:

> There are no dinosaurs left, simply because they were unable
> to adapt to changing environmental conditions. We doctors
> are now faced with the greatest revolution in the allocation of
> medical care since the time of Hippocrates, yet we, too, are
> presently milling about ponderously, waiting for the old water-
> ing holes to refill. They never will. . . .
>
> We stand a much better chance of preserving our profes-
> sionalism through the process of becoming unionized work-
> ers—admittedly a terribly unprofessional thing to do, by my
> own estimation, just a few short years ago. But then, that's just
> the sort of adaptation those now-extinct dinosaurs were incapa-
> ble of making, isn't it? (1984b:41–44)

It is difficult to determine whether the increase in the number of
problems members were bringing to the UAPD was an artifact of
expanding membership or whether there were in fact more instances
when physicians were being treated "unfairly." News items in the
UAPD newsletter tend to support Dr. Marcus's assessment that doctors were, in fact, encountering increased pressure. The union intervened on behalf of doctors confronting a wide range of problems in
their dealings with a growing number of health sector organizations.

In one instance, the union filed a grievance against the Fountain
Valley Community Hospital administrator after an anesthesiologist
was told, "Your name is no longer on the schedule." The grievance

noted that the administrator could not take this step without the approval of the medical staff. The doctor was reinstated.

The union became involved when one hospital decided to purchase another, St. Joseph's. It then proceeded to dismiss all the physicians associated with St. Joseph's. The UAPD entered into the matter to represent them because they had not been consulted in the transaction. The union argued that their due process rights had been violated since St. Joseph's had entered into contractual arrangements with the doctors on staff. The UAPD succeeded in bringing all the parties to the table to work out the arrangements.

In another case, the administrator of a hospital with financial difficulties decided to retroactively change the reimbursement formula for distributing funds to the physicians. He announced that in light of the crisis, the hospital would "back bill" physicians. The UAPD convinced the administrator not to take this step unilaterally.

One UAPD member kept the California State Surveillance team from inspecting the files of his inner-city patients. The union's participation forced a change in procedures, preventing Medicaid investigations throughout the state.

The union leadership defines these cases as relatively easy wins. The organizations had taken steps that were clearly inappropriate and would not have been upheld in court—and they knew it. Administrators were accustomed to negotiating with individual doctors who had little experience dealing with the new realities and even less experience in addressing them collectively. These administrators discovered that they would have to respond differently to the UAPD, which brought to the negotiations an established record of experience, was persistent, and was prepared to take legal action. At the end of the 1970s, Dr. Marcus summed up the UAPD's growing reputation for winning battles with the assertion that it was now well enough established to be considered a mature union (Letter to members, February 1979).

In a letter to members reviewing the union's first ten years, Dr. Marcus reported the following accomplishments. The UAPD had recently opened a third office in Sacramento, in addition to the ones in San Francisco and Los Angeles. It had a full-time staff of 14. Over the past year or so it had installed a new telephone system, developed in-house printing capability, and purchased a new computer system. It reported an income in 1981 of $642,000 and expenditures of $647,000 (Letter to members, June 1982).

The UAPD's record stood in sharp contrast to that of other physicians' unions. The national federation had disintegrated in the mid-1970s. During the latter half of the 1970s the UAPD agreed to allow other unions to affiliate. By 1980 the UAPD listed 10,000 members, associated with affiliates in 16 states.

The federation of UAPD affiliates met in San Francisco in October 1980 and again in March 1981, to hammer out a position statement on where the union movement stood on various issues confronting physicians and dentists. It turned out that the affiliates brought to these meetings vastly different priorities, levels of experience, and commitment. Since the federated structure permitted the affiliates complete freedom to define their issues and determine their approaches, the unions found it impossible to coalesce. There was no single overriding issue to unify doctors from different regions of the country. Although increasing government intervention was the primary focus of concern, the impact varied from region to region. Not only did hospitals, state Medicaid agencies, Medicare carriers, and other third parties vary in how they implemented the directives; the doctors affected also differed in how strongly they felt about the results.

An account of the rise and decline of the physicians' union movement appeared in a 1983 issue of *Medical Economics* (Holoweiko). The movement could claim a membership of about 55,000 in 1974, but had begun to fade within the next two years. Holoweiko noted that the UAPD was the only major doctors' union to have survived, and asked Dr. Marcus why. Dr. Marcus replied that the movement declined because national health insurance proposals had evaporated and physicians were doing well economically. He added that, while the UAPD appeared to have declined in size, it was actually only divesting itself of its affiliates. Its core membership in California was 7,000 as of 1982 and promised to double by the end of 1983. (Because affiliates continued to come and go, membership figures have varied widely over the years. The UAPD has never issued an official membership count.)

The UAPD represented physicians in their dealings with a variety of organizations, in both the public and private sectors. In many cases the actions the union took on behalf of its membership also benefited doctors who were not members. The entity with which the UAPD has had the most sustained record of interaction is the state of California.

The UAPD Battles the State of California

Dr. Marcus made clear his attitude toward the ever-increasing number of plans and agencies involved in overseeing quality of care: "All the recent nonsense about 'peer review' and 'quality assurance' is simply Orwellian Newspeak for 'Keep it cheap, or else!'" (1984b:43) He rejected the idea that doctors maintain control over the practice of medicine because control over their work remains in the hands of fellow physicians—peers. "A peer, by definition, is an equal in rank or merit. The new 'peer reviewers' are simply hired hands whose job security is dependent on their ability to cut costs by denying care to our patients and enhancing profit margins for the bosses who pay their salaries. Call them overlords or commissars, if you will, but stop playing word games—they are no longer our peers!" (1984b:43).

UAPD staff members say that they repeatedly heard about members' problems with the Board of Medical Quality Assurance (BMQA). Formerly the California State Licensure Board, the BMQA's stated function was upholding medical practice standards and overseeing the medical licensure. The UAPD did not see it that way. In a 1980 letter in the form of a brochure to the membership, Dr. Marcus said that the union was considering legal action against the BMQA. He noted that the Board had changed from being an agency under the medical profession's auspices to one that included lay persons. The agency was now primarily committed to identifying fraudulent behavior by physicians, and Dr. Marcus contended that it did so in an unprofessional and personally destructive manner.

The union's position was that the BMQA's actions were inappropriate on legal and procedural grounds. In one instance, Dr. Marcus described the case of a physician who was told that he had been accused of improper behavior and that there would be an informal hearing before any other action would be taken. The representative of the Board behaved in a way that resulted in everyone in the hospital knowing in advance that the doctor was being investigated, even if no one, including the doctor, had been told the nature of the problem being investigated (Letter to members, April 3, 1979).

The agency also created a Special Investigator position, which the UAPD tried to have abolished (*UAPD Newsletter*, June 12, 1980). The investigators were assigned to watch doctors, though it is not entirely clear what they were expected to find. The investigators' zeal to find something appears to have been excessive; one was caught with binoculars in a tree on the grounds of a state mental hospital (*UAPD Newsletter*, February 14, 1980). State authorities were embarrassed and agreed to curtail such activities.

According to UAPD staff, however, they were apparently not sufficiently embarrassed to review their policies. Within the next few months, the BMQA sent an investigator to check on unspecified charges made by an unnamed accuser. The physician involved insisted on having a union representative present. In settling the UAPD law suit against the Surveillance and Utilization Review (SUR) Program of the state Medicaid program, the state issued regulations to the effect that the SUR would provide advance notice of inspections and permit union representatives to be present (*UAPD Newsletter*, February 14, 1980). The investigator tried to coerce the UAPD representative to talk privately and off the record in the hope that she might reveal incriminating evidence. The UAPD threatened to retaliate, stating, "Their tactics are alien to American concepts of due process, but they continue to build secret dossiers on the doctors of California, and to bully and coerce them" (*UAPD Newsletter*, April 30, 1980).

Ironically, when Governor Jerry Brown decided to withdraw the Board of Medical Quality Assurance (which continued to function as the state licensing agency) from the Federation of State Medical Boards, the UAPD felt it had no alternative but to oppose the plan. Brown had made clear that he planned to create an alternative agency that he could shape to fulfill his own agenda, namely, to reduce physicians' practice privileges, by broadening the pool of those permitted to prescribe medications and perform invasive procedures. The UAPD argued that the BMQA should be retained (*UAPD Newsletter*, February 12, 1981). Brown's proposal failed to gain much support from the California legislature.

In 1981 the governor apparently "signed into a bill requiring physicians to report to the authorities all sexually active females under 18 who are unmarried." The union newsletter had this to say:

> Designed to protect minors from sexual abuse, this sloppily-drawn bill mandates a total breach of confidentiality, drives minor females away from needed medical care, and, in general, lowers the diminishing reservoir of respect for the legislative process. The UAPD has contacted every legislator and your governor, and notified all California media to hasten repeal of this misbegotten law, before we are all drowned in the laughter it generates (*UAPD Newsletter,* February 12, 1981)

Another entity with which California doctors have had continuing disagreements is the state agency that administers Medicaid, known as Medi-Cal. The UAPD has engaged in many battles with Medi-Cal, and the union has not always come out the winner. For example, the UAPD lost its 1983 suit against Santa Clara County over care for those who are poor but not eligible for Medi-Cal. The county refused to pay for the care of indigent patients. It announced to all doctors practicing in the county that they would be expected to donate free medical care to the indigent and threatened them with misdemeanor prosecution if they failed to do so (*UAPD Newsletter,* December 1983). When the union lost this appeal, it participated in authoring a bill, designed to apply to county governments throughout the state, that would obligate them to pay physicians for indigent health care when a county failed to meet its statutory obligation to furnish indigent care (*UAPD Newsletter,* May 9, 1984). The bill passed.

In another case, the union took the State of California to court, charging that the Surveillance and Utilization Review Board (SUR), created by the state to monitor Medi-Cal reimbursement, was flagrantly breaching its agreement with doctors. The UAPD objected to SUR's practice of reporting doctors to BMQA prior to filing any charges. Doctors were in jeopardy of losing their licenses before an official complaint had been filed and before they had an opportunity to respond. The UAPD succeeded in having the court prohibit this behavior (*UAPD Newsletter,* April 30, 1980).

The UAPD repeatedly tried to get the legislature to increase Medi-Cal fees or at least to prevent fee cuts (*UAPD Newsletter,* May

9, 1984). One of the union's earliest efforts to affect the legislative process took placed in 1975 when the state proposed to alter the Medi-Cal reimbursement system. A UAPD member testified that there were "massive errors" in the statistical data base developed by fiscal intermediaries to set doctors' fees. He charged that the plan underestimated the increase in the cost of living, using a 35 percent figure rather than the more accurate 51.9 percent; that it incorrectly assessed the malpractice insurance rate at 1 percent rather than 5 to 10 percent of a physician's gross income; and, finally, that it set fees at least 12 percent below where they should have been at the start of the program (*UAPD Newsletter*, January 1975). The UAPD did alter the state's commitment to impose an arbitrary cap on physician reimbursement, but it was unable to convince the legislature not to cut some specific Medi-Cal services, such as psychiatric and dental services (*UAPD Newsletter*, June 1982).

Since the union could not count on negotiations and appeals to the legislature, it repeatedly found that it had to resort to the courts to address problems with Medi-Cal procedures. In one instance, the UAPD filed a petition with the State Office of Administrative Law asking it to review two aspects of the Medi-Cal audit method employed by the Department of Health Services (*UAPD Newsletter*, April 1987). The UAPD argued that "the Department of Health Services regularly uses definitions above and beyond the RVS (relative value scale) code definitions to determine documentation requirements for Medi-Cal providers. Those definitions were never subject to public hearing and review, and none of the procedural protections that go into adopting a regulation were provided to providers. . . ." In essence, physicians did not know what the reimbursement rules were because they had not been published. The UAPD won these cases on administrative grounds, since the state's bureaucratic procedures must be put in writing to be legitimate. When the state failed to acknowledge the ruling, the UAPD filed another suit, which had the effect of changing the procedure but not the number of audits (*UAPD Newsletter*, May 1988).

In 1986, a new Medi-Cal Deputy Director of Audit and Investigation took office. He decided to increase the number and alter the kind of audits his department would undertake. He established a quota of 1,000 audits. However, he could not identify enough physicians who would meet the minimum reimbursement criteria outlined in audit guidelines, so he lowered the minimum to $10,000 per year of Medi-Cal billings. When that limit failed to identify many more physicians who could be audited, he turned to random audits of ten percent of Medi-Cal providers.

Physicians object to audits, according to the head of the UAPD Practice Management Department (the reorganized and expanded Insurance Grievance Department), because they are costly, time-consuming, and disruptive. They also bring increased risk of additional audits. An audit by one government agency can touch off a series of new audits by any number of other agencies because the agencies are permitted to exchange information. (They are not required to report such exchanges, so it is never entirely clear whether such an exchange of information has prompted an audit.) Medi-Cal auditors are permitted to contact agencies such as the IRS, the Health Care Financing Administration (which administers Medicare), the State Department of Labor with regard to treatment of employees, agencies concerned with public health and sanitation matters, and so on.

In October 1988, the UAPD announced that the Medi-Cal case had been settled when the agency agreed to do "informational audits" rather than punitive audits. The judge decreed that ". . . only members of the UAPD can file claims against the Department of Health Services over the department's improper audit techniques. All audits of UAPD members concluded before May 15, 1988 were declared invalid. The department estimates that as much as $31 million may be reimbursed to physicians as the result of this decision" (*UAPD Newsletter*, October 1988).

The union was not able to prevent passage of a bill requiring physicians accused of a felony to be reported to the Medical Board of California, the reorganized version of the BMQA. Since the felony did not have to be related to medical practice, accusations related to tax matters, participation in political demonstrations, or hiding undocumented aliens in churches would put the physician at risk of losing his or her license. The law gave absolute immunity to the accuser even if he or she knowingly made false charges. The intent of the law was to preserve the "inviolate character of peer review" (*UAPD Newsletter*, December 1990).

In 1991 a bill which would have given the Medical Board wire-tapping authority was introduced. Although it did not pass, the UAPD expected proponents to resubmit the bill in the future (*UAPD Newsletter*, November 1991).

Clearly, the UAPD's monitoring of the legislature provides a valuable service. Some bills are crucial to a particular sector of the membership, and others are simply likely to be bothersome to many.

"Doctor Substitute" Legislation

The UAPD undertook a major battle in the early 1980s in response to Governor Brown's campaign to permit allied health workers to carry out work traditionally viewed as the exclusive prerogative of doctors. Brown launched a continuing barrage of proposals that came to be known as "doctor substitute" laws. (His successors favored similar initiatives, but did not pursue them quite as vigorously.) The statutory amendments Brown proposed would have permitted allied health personnel, i.e., nurses and such groups as psychologists and chiropractors to admit patients to all acute care hospitals; to prescribe medications, diagnose, order tests, and determine therapy; and to replace the attending physician (*UAPD Newsletter*, August 22, 1979). The April 30, 1980 *UAPD Newsletter* announced, ". . . [T]he new Title 22 regulations governing Nurse Practitioners have been published, and they represent a partial victory for the intensive opposition mounted by the UAPD. Gone are the provisions allowing nurses to be designated 'attending practitioners,' with virtual carte blanche approval to treat patients as their own in hospitals."

The UAPD continued to object to changes that remained in the statute, including the effort to define standard procedures and the ceding of control over patients to a committee that could bypass control by physicians. Attorney General George Deukmejian eventually ruled that nurses who prescribe medications are violating the Medical Practices Act. Jerry Brown's appointee to head the Department of Health Services responded by setting aside the ruling, claiming it was only advisory (*UAPD Newsletter*, May 5, 1981).

Similarly a "denturist" clinic in Sacramento had been allowed to fit and dispense dental prostheses in violation of state law until the UAPD demanded it be closed. The California State Board of Dental

Examiners took action only when the UAPD began proceedings to sue (*UAPD Newsletter*, February 14, 1980).

Two bills to expand the scope of practice of registered nurses and nurse practitioners, allowing them to prescribe and dispense medications, were passed in the 1984 legislative session (*UAPD Newsletter*, March 30, 1984). Extension of nurses' right to prescribe came up again in 1985, together with a bill to include chiropractors as personal physicians for purposes of worker's compensation (*UAPD Newsletter*, March 1985). The UAPD opposed it again. The issue continues to come up and continues to be unsettled.

In 1982 a State Senate budget committee passed language greatly expanding the authority of psychologists in state Department of Mental Health hospitals. The UAPD newsletter warned that if the bill became law, it would permit psychologists to fill vacant psychiatrist positions, and encouraged physicians to oppose the legislation (*UAPD Newsletter*, April 1982). The proposed legislation did not pass.

In 1985, the California Association of Psychology Providers won a suit, known as *CAPP vs. Rank*, to permit them to diagnose, admit to hospitals, and treat patients independently of psychiatrists. As a result, the Department of Health Services proposed to revise the regulations. The UAPD submitted a position paper quoting the director of the Department of Mental Health, who stated that the biological basis of mental illness was being rediscovered, and arguing that viewing psychologists as capable of making diagnoses was "based on an out-of-date concept of mental illness, rooted in the state of knowledge as it existed prior to the 1960s" (*UAPD Newsletter*, December 1985). The court ruled in favor of the psychologists (*UAPD Newsletter*, June 1986). The California Supreme Court accepted the case for review in 1988, and the UAPD filed an *amicus* brief (*UAPD Newsletter*, January 1988). Under the heading "Important Victory!" a special insertion in the June 1988 *UAPD Newsletter* quoted from the ruling against psychologists: "It is clear that while a physician's function may encompass the practice of psychology the converse is not true; i.e., a psychologist may not practice medicine. It is this distinction and difference which lies at the heart of the issue. . . ."

There have also been circumstances in which the UAPD sided with other health care workers. In one case, the union made available to the press a strong letter of support for the California Nurses Association (CNA), which was actively opposing an AMA plan to create a new cadre of workers, "registered care technologists," to take over some nursing duties. The president of the CNA, Marilyn Rogers, sent a letter (July 9, 1988) thanking Dr. Marcus for the following comments.

> Professional nurses are an integral part of the excellence of today's health care, and they deserve the unqualified support of all physicians. If the AMA is sincere in wanting to increase the numbers of nurses . . . may we suggest to the AMA that they use what has always been the most reliable inducement of all— support of the quest by nurses for much-needed reliable improvements in their wages, hours, and working conditions.

The UAPD has generally supported health care workers in their demands for better wages and working conditions in negotiations with hospitals. The support has been verbal. The union has never advocated participation in job actions initiated by other health care workers.

Dealings with Other Organizations

The UAPD fought the city of San Francisco for years over a miscalculation in the formula the city used to pay salaried physicians. The union won a class action lawsuit, first filed in 1978, with a $15 million award to the plaintiffs in 1982. The city lost on appeal but continued to stall (Letter to membership, February 25, 1983). The city began to pay out the monies only after a new mayor came into office in 1986. By that time the accumulated interest cost the city far more than the original $15 million settlement (account by Gary Robinson).

On occasion, the UAPD went to court to prevent non-government third-party payers from taking unilateral actions that would have detrimental effects on doctors. The union sued when Blue Cross announced that it intended to transfer some of its subscribers to its Prudent Buyer PPO (preferred provider organization, composed of health care delivery organizations that agreed to accept standardized reimbursements set by Blue Cross). The UAPD charged Blue Cross with breach of contract, failing to negotiate, and violation of anti-trust laws (*UAPD Newsletter*, October 16, 1984). The California Superior Court ultimately found in favor of the UAPD.

In 1977, when Dr. Weinmann, current president of the UAPD, headed a local unit of the union, he devoted considerable energy to fighting the billing practices used by Stanford University hospitals. He charged that Stanford was double-billing Medicare—once for hospital care and once for care by a senior physician, when interns and residents actually treated patients. In some departments, the name of the department head was used as a matter of course even if the department head never looked at the patient's chart.

Dr. Weinmann recalls that few of his colleagues appreciated the reasons behind this campaign. His point, he says, was that cutting down on double-billing at Stanford and other medical centers across the country would save far more money than the continual nitpicking harassment of individual physicians over billing. Moreover, Stanford was claiming for itself money that should have been paid to physicians. In the end, he succeeded in having Stanford's practices corrected. Stanford representatives told the press they had agreed to repay Medicare $1.5 million, but Dr. Weinmann says they paid over three times that amount.

Lawsuits on Behalf of Individuals

The UAPD generally did not become involved in suits initiated by individual members. It avoided all cases involving criminal charges. However, according to Gary Robinson, the union agreed to pursue legal action on behalf of individual members when the cases had the potential to set precedents. It chose the cases carefully, preferring to limit them to administrative procedural issues. An example is a case filed against the City of San Francisco in 1978, in which a member was denied retirement and other benefits. The union won benefits retroactive to 1954, establishing a precedent that would benefit other doctors who were city employees. Similarly, the UAPD was prepared to sue Fresno Community Hospital on behalf of a member who was denied permission to see his personnel file. The administrator agreed to release the files.

The UAPD submitted an *amicus* brief when the Board of Medical

Quality Assurance accused a UAPD member of incompetence. He was charged with not using the full array of cardiac monitoring techniques in the treatment of an eighty-eight-year-old patient. The Board asserted that he should have treated the patient more aggressively. When the doctor argued that his treatment plan was appropriate, the BMQA held that it was authorized to determine the standard of care that would apply. The court ruled in favor of the physician. The court held that there may be dispute about how aggressive therapy should be under certain circumstances within the profession, but the Board was not authorized to supercede the standards of the profession it regulates.

The UAPD presented the ruling as a victory for all physicians, who could have reasonable disagreements about treatment without having to consider the risk of harassment by the BMQA. From the perspective of the UAPD, physicians accused of inappropriate behavior had few alternatives other than going to court in light of the BMQA's stance; therefore the union announced that it would offer whatever support it could to members in good standing (*UAPD Newsletter*, April 1987).

The UAPD has been willing to take on a variety of causes on behalf of its membership, it has won a large share of those battles. The question is, why do members feel that they need the UAPD to fight their battles? Why can't they turn to other mechanisms and organizations, especially their professional associations, to provide the same services? I turn to the differences between the UAPD and professional associations in the following chapter.

❧ 10 ☙
Why a Union and Not a
Professional Association?

D r. Marcus's view of the American Medical Association (AMA) is summed up in a 1983 interview with the journal *Medical Economics:* "Physicians have been drawn to us because the AMA and its state societies have done nothing but retreat and wring their hands. . . . [They are] toothless fogies who clutter up the socioeconomic battlefield" (Holoweiko, 1983:210).[1]

It took some time and many discussions with the AMA leadership before Dr. Marcus took this stance. When he began to organize the UAPD, he turned to the AMA leadership to explore the possibilities of mutual support and cooperation. They told him that the AMA was already serving its members well, so there was no need for a physicians' union. Furthermore, he was told, the medical societies can, if the members wish, provide additional services comparable to those the union intended to provide. Initially, Dr. Marcus hoped that he could convince the AMA to change its position. In the December 1972 *UAPD Newsletter,* he wrote, "If the Medical Societies then take over what the Union has originated, none of us has lost anything."

But over the next year or so the AMA leadership made it clear that the AMA would neither assist the physicians' union movement nor take up any of the causes the movement had espoused. An editorial in the April 1973 AMA newsletter called physicians' unions "divisive and counterproductive to the needs of the profession" ("Unions

---

[1] Membership in the AMA has dropped dramatically since the Golden Age of Medicine. The AMA claims that 40 percent of all doctors are currently members (Oberman, 1993). If interns and residents are excluded, then it has enrolled only about 33 percent of all doctors during the last two decades (Budrys, 1986:31–33).

Opposed," 1973). The editorial claimed that professional associations, unlike unions, place the public welfare before the economic
interests of their members. Unionism, it argued, requires collective
action and the suppression of individual rights, whereas the protection of individualism and professional freedom by professional associations serves the "professional man as well as the public welfare."

The debate over physicians' unions vs. the AMA had come up
before. One of the earliest discussions in print appeared in 1941.
The author argued that the AMA should become a union, since
unions were exempt from constraint of trade legislation (Richardson,
1941). As early as 1956, a North Carolina physician argued that
unionization was necessary to combat the inroads of third parties,
including insurance companies and industry (quoted in Burton,
1972:110). The AMA took no notice of such arguments until the
early 1970s, when it could no longer ignore the subject because
members who were in a position to step up to the AMA's public
platform kept bringing it up. Dr. Stanley Peterson, president of the
newly formed Federation of Physicians and Dentists, was particularly
interested in calling the attention of organized medicine to the question of unionization. As a delegate to the 1973 AMA convention, he
made a formal proposal that the AMA establish guidelines for collective bargaining. While the convention refused to do so, the delegates
were forced into an extended and public discussion of physician
unionization because Peterson continued to agitate for it.

The 1973 AMA meetings ended with the House of Delegates
deciding to issue a condemnation of physicians' unions. Dr. Marcus
interpreted this stance to the UAPD membership:

> I believe that the AMA regards itself in a desperate situation
> with regard to its failure to attract new members and its losing
> old members. I feel that it regards us as somewhat of a
> threat. . . .
>   The AMA, unfortunately, has always been a responding
> type of organization, waiting for the course of history and
> course of sociology to bypass it, and then responding with sort
> of studied moderation to things that already happened. We
> have no intention of being the goad or gadfly to stimulate the
> AMA into the type of activity it should have been doing all

along. I spoke to Dr. Roth [AMA president] and I told him, at
one point, even if the AMA decided to become more militant
in the representation of physicians, he could depend on the
fact that unions were simply not going to pack up their tents
and steal away—that we are around for keeps, and that they
are going to have to reconcile themselves to living alongside
us, harmoniously. (Ulrich, 1973:65)

Thus after being firmly and repeatedly rebuffed by the AMA, Dr.
Marcus changed his stance. He would no longer seek to alter the
AMA's thinking about physicians' unions. Nor was he interested in
defeating the AMA. Instead, he wanted to clarify the differences
between what the AMA could offer to doctors and what a union
could offer: "We have stated repeatedly that we support the AMA in
its scientific, professional and educational endeavors, but that a parallel arm of medicine—the unions—must provide the specialized
power we need immediately in the socio-economic arena" (1973:5).

A doctor who had recently joined the UAPD explained his different experiences with the AMA and with the union:

When a hospital chain assumed the direction of one of the
hospitals which we [radiology group] service, it was rumored
that we would no longer be allowed to continue under the
agreement that we had negotiated with the advent of Medicare.
. . . I can remember writing to both the AMA and the ACR
[American College of Radiology]. . . . Neither organization
tried to analyze my particular situation but gave generalized
advice along with the old standard of "consult your own attorney." . . . [T]he union . . . immediately sent a representative . . .
and met with our physician members, gathered the complaints
of the physicians, and together we chartered a plan of action.

To cite another case, we were recently sent reams of new
forms. . . . Our office manager could not convince the responsible people that this change meant more work for both ourselves and the agencies involved. . . . On the same day the
union office was notified. . . . [T]he union informed us that one
of their personnel had contacted a specific person at the MIO
[Medi-Cal Intermediary Operations] office. We were then in-

structed by the MIO that there was no problem. . . . (*UAPD Newsletter*, November 1973)

The author of the letter concludes, "Gentlemen, no matter what is said about the nonprofessionalism of unions, they can be your right arm and they can plead your case convincingly without resorting to gutter tactics."

No argument, apparently, was strong enough to convince the AMA to reconsider its position during the early 1970s. The AMA stated in print on more than one occasion that it would not and could not become a trade union ("The AMA Is Not . . . ," 1972). Curiously, some AMA representatives took personally the increasing interest in doctors' unions. Bernard Hirsch, AMA counsel during the early 1970s, implied that the AMA's organizational feelings had been hurt: "How would you feel if somebody moved into your house, took over your bedrooms, bathrooms and kitchen and said 'You can have the closet'? It is our house to begin with and they are trying to shove us out" (de Grandpre, 1973:802).

Over time, the AMA became less willing to get its feelings hurt without hitting back. More than one UAPD staff member recalled the AMA's efforts to make life difficult for the union. It seems that the AMA turned to the Federal Trade Commission (FTC) to complain that the UAPD was engaged in collective bargaining on behalf of physicians in private practice (Meyer, 1989b). The FTC treats private practice physicians as independent contractors engaged in operating small businesses and prohibits them from bargaining collectively, but in this instance they investigated and determined that there was no case to pursue because the UAPD was not actually engaged in collective bargaining over wages and salaries. One of the UAPD's organizers nonetheless says he now enjoys attending a regularly scheduled health lawyers' national seminar where the FTC attorneys outline their anti-trust policy on organizing physicians based on the results of their investigation of the UAPD.

Other UAPD staff members suspect that the AMA had something to do with investigations by the Internal Revenue Service, the California Department of Labor, and other government agencies. They express pride that none of the investigations ever led to negative findings of any sort.

The AMA Response—Negotiation without Unionization

Although the physicians' union movement had gone into decline by the latter half of the 1970s, this was the point at which the AMA decided to address the concerns unions had raised. The AMA established a Department of Negotiations to teach physicians how to bargain. According to the AMA's executive director, the Department was created to provide doctors with "impasse-resolving machinery" (Sammons, 1976). To justify the AMA's interest in bargaining strategies, he said that "physicians were being forced to engage in negotiations because hospital employees were becoming unionized and their demands were infringing on physicians' ability to function in the hospital" (Sammons, 1976:113).

The AMA put on seminars featuring labor organizers, industrial psychologists, and labor attorneys, as well as AMA attorneys. Apparently a great deal of time was spent on questions about doctors' unions (Steele, 1976). Interestingly, the AMA announced that it was holding seminars across the entire country, but of the first six, two were planned for California. The Negotiations Department reportedly took a "distinctly anti-union tone" in the seminars. The head of the department encouraged physicians to be aware of union activity in their environment "to learn why these dues-ghouls are making headway. Often, if caught early enough, the cancer can be forestalled."

The Negotiations Department, which had been announced with some fanfare, was allowed to fade out in 1981 without much said about its accomplishments (UAPD Newsletter, August 1981). The American Medical News, the AMA's weekly newsletter, continued to offer advice on negotiations from time to time over the next few years. Recently, the AMA has again begun to express interest in helping doctors negotiate, offering members advice on entering into contractual agreements. The American Medical News has carried an increasing number of stories about the negotiation process, reported individuals' experiences, and carried technical articles identifying language and clauses about which physicians should be wary (Johnsson, 1993; McCormick, 1993b, 1992).

The AMA seems to have accepted the fact that physicians are no longer in a position to practice without entering into contracts with various third-party payers and health care delivery organizations. Until this time, it preferred to use its resources to oppose the expansion of pre-paid care systems, tacitly discouraging physicians from participating in such arrangements. In 1993, however, the AMA made the following announcement:

> The Association is "turning itself upside-down" to make the AMA "the physician resource" on managed care issues, says General Counsel Kirk Johnson. The linchpin of the program is a network of expert consultants who will be on call to provide physicians with one-on-one practical advice.
>
> The AMA has not historically been a strong proponent of HMOs or other types of managed care. . . . But that attitude has changed markedly in recent years. . . . Medicine's change in attitude has been driven in part by changing practice patterns. In 1992, seven of 10 physicians derived at least some income from managed care. And physician participation in managed care is expected to rise drastically if the health care system is reformed on a managed care competition model. (McCormick, 1993)

Whether the AMA succeeds in becoming a resource on negotiating with HMOs remains to be seen. It has been reluctant to become involved in the problems of individual members in the past because so many disagreements pitted doctors against each other. The AMA refused to take a stand in such disputes and recommended that the parties engage their own attorneys. Negotiations between doctors and institutions are being viewed differently, however, even when the individuals negotiating on behalf of the institutions are doctors.

The forces operating to press the AMA into opting for collective solutions continue to mount. In a 1992 AMA survey of 1,003 physicians, 82 percent said that doctors should have a negotiating agent who bargains with the government over fees ("Stats," 1992).[2] In late 1992, executive vice president James Todd wrote to every member

---

[2] An earlier study by a private consulting firm found that "55% of physicians said they would consider joining a physicians union even if it only provided a forum for their viewpoints." Surgeons were more favorably disposed to joining (Jensen, 1987:64).

of the Senate and the House seeking support for antitrust law reform (McCormick, 1992). This is consistent with the AMA's new drive to obtain government permission for physicians to engage in collective bargaining. The AMA calls this a request for a "level playing field" that would allow physicians to negotiate with large insurers.

By law neither the AMA nor state medical associations can engage in the same activities as a union. Thus, to say that neither the AMA nor the California Medical Association could become a union is accurate, at least not without altering their respective legal statuses or charters.

One restriction that particularly hampers some professional organizations is found in Section 501(c)(3) of the Internal Revenue Code. This statute prohibits associations established as technical and scientific societies from engaging in political activities with the aim of influencing legislation. Thus, the specialty societies mount educational meetings but do not lobby. Professional associations like the AMA that are classified under Section 501(c)(6) may engage in political activities but may not bargain over fees and wages.

The AMA finds itself approaching a new frontier that looks very much like the territory in which the UAPD is well established. It is just beginning to explore problems that the union has addressed over many years (Johnsson, 1993; McCormick, 1993c, 1992). The staff and officers of the UAPD say the AMA has a great deal to learn. They are, however, convinced that the AMA will not succeed no matter how hard it tries. As one staff representative put it, what doctor in California would be willing to wait to consult with someone in Chicago about a problem that the person in Chicago couldn't possibly know anything about? Being well enough informed to assist doctors across the country with their problems is just not possible. Moreover, assisting each individual who asks for advice could easily overwhelm the resources of even an organization as rich and powerful as the AMA.

California Medical Association and Its Alternative Union

UAPD staff members are certain that the California state medical society is not likely to make the union obsolete. Gary Robinson says, "I would say that between around 1972 and 1984, you could count on one hand the good ideas that the CMA [California Medical Association] had. In the last seven or eight years they have become much smarter, much more modern in their ideas." In Dr. Weinmann's view, "We benefited hugely from their slothfulness and torpor, not to mention the stupidity that was behind it."

To illustrate, Dr. Weinmann related this tale:

> The CMA awarded a prize to the president of Life Guard, which is one of the leading HMOs that competes with Kaiser. It [the HMO] had developed a set of contracts that were universally despised by the doctors. . . . [W]e were taking the same organization to court. Many of the doctors understood then that there really was a difference between the physicians' union and the medical association. So when they gave him that award, we got a few new members.

However, Dr. Weinmann concurred with Gary Robinson's assessment that the CMA is far more sophisticated than the AMA. In fact, he noted that in recent years the union has had an excellent relationship with the CMA on lobbying. On a few occasions the CMA even lent its lobbyist to the union when it was scheduled to testify before the legislature.

In any case, legal restrictions were not enough to stop the CMA from attempting to set up a competing union. The CMA created the Public Practice Bureau in 1979 through which it intended to displace the UAPD. By the end of the year the Public Practice Bureau had attracted seven dues-paying members. The UAPD estimates that the CMA spent approximately $12,000 on legal fees, staff, postage, and other costs to recruit *each* of the seven physicians it was ultimately able to attract (*UAPD Newsletter*, December 12, 1980).

According to Gary Robinson, the CMA went about recruiting to its version of a union by appropriating the UAPD's wording from the header of its newsletter. It even used the same typeface. The Bureau took the same stance on issues that the UAPD did. The UAPD's reaction was to file an unfair labor practice charge listing two complaints: one, against the state for giving preferential treatment to the CMA, and two, against the CMA for using illegal and dishonest organizing tactics (*UAPD Newsletter*, June 12, 1980). Once the state looked into the complaint, it threatened to revoke the CMA's quasi-governmental privileges (its role in setting licensing and peer review standards) if it chose to alter its status from professional association to labor union without altering its state charter. The fact that the charges were upheld contributed to the demise of the CMA's ill-conceived offspring.

Whether the CMA was motivated by the UAPD's complaints against it or simply out of anger over its defeat in the battle for recruits, the association chose to retaliate. The CMA threw its political support to another union, the California State Employees Association, which was actively engaged in organizing doctors into multi-occupational bargaining units. Gary Robinson said, "They just discredited themselves because all along they were saying that doctors need to have separate representation. The California Medical Association just ended up looking silly."

Why Do Doctors Say They Join Unions?

It appears that doctors who join unions do not see themselves as radicals seeking to change the system, but rather as conservatives seeking to preserve medical professionalism. In one study carried out in the early 1970s, unionized doctors offered the following reasons for joining: the need to protect their interests and those of their patients; fear of legislation that would permit insurance companies to decide which services would be approved; the need for an organization that could ensure the right to set fees, work rules, and other regulations to provide proper care of patients (Bognanno, Dworkin, and Fashoyin, 1975).

A few years later, another group of researchers reported virtually the same results. Physicians said they joined to preserve their freedom to practice medicine according to their professional judgment. By the same token, those opposed to unions said they did not believe a union could represent their interests any better than existing professional associations (Klover, Stephens, and Luchsinger, 1980).

While the symbolic meanings attached to collective bargaining may still not be entirely consistent with the presentation of themselves and their work interests that professionals and white collar workers want to project, they have been joining unions in increasing

numbers (Hirsch and McPherson, 1993). In 1994, the rate of unionization among professionals was 26.8 percent, the vast majority of
these union members being in the public sector (U.S. Department
of Labor, 1995:216).[3] Professionals and white collar workers, and the
associations they join, are pursuing aims similar to those of unions
and their blue collar members. They are both certainly interested in
"bread and butter" issues—higher wages and better benefits. Beyond
that, associations and unions share an interest in enhancing the opportunities available to their members. Both union and professional
association leaders lament that they are losing influence over social
policies that govern the members' conditions of work (Hoffman,
1976).

What, then, becomes of the essential differences between the
work and working conditions of laborers and white collar or professional workers (Cook, et al. 1978)? What does moving from a cottage industry to a modern health care system mean for doctors? Will
they really go through a process of work reorganization that parallels
industrialization? The next chapter will examine the industrialization
process so as to enable us to compare it with the changes being
implemented in the health care sector.

[3] Private sector professionals have exhibited far less interest in unionization than public
sector employees (Edwards, 1993). Only one in ten private sector professionals is involved
in collective bargaining. Public sector professionals have an established record of benefiting to a greater degree from collective bargaining than do private sector professionals
(Jackson and Clark, 1987).

⚔ 11 ⚑

From Cottage Industry to
the Modern Era:
The Industrialization Model

During the early 1980s Dr. Marcus turned his attention to the corporate takeover of the health care sector, which, he acknowledged, had, until then, indeed been a "cottage industry."[1] In his view, the move out of the cottage industry stage of production to a more modern stage, as orchestrated by those who have much to gain, left doctors confused and disturbed with no place to turn (1986:4). He described the changing conditions as follows:

> As a necessary prelude to this corporate takeover by the so-called medical-industrial complex of what essentially has been a cottage industry that has always operated on a piecework basis, it has become necessary for this newly emerging managerial class to capture control of the medical profession; . . . [V]enture-capitalist types perceived that there were fortunes to be made from the marketing of medical care; so all of this cant about there being a "health care cost crisis" is simply a pretext to enable them to make their fortunes. (1986b:403)

He went on to say that the venture capitalists gained control over the health sector by convincing the public that doctors were responsible for the crisis. "Doctors have been proclaimed too rich, uncaring, negligent, incompetent, unavailable, venal, lecherous and inter-

---

[1] Medicine's shift from the "cottage industry" stage to a modern stage has been mentioned in passing by a number of observers, including Marmor, Schlesinger, and Smithey, 1987; Jellinek and Nurcombe, 1993; Larkin, 1993.

ested only in money; they don't make house calls, they commit malpractice, they perform unnecessary surgery, and [they] themselves constitute the greatest obstacles to decent patient care. . . ."

Corporatization and Proletarianization

Some observers have predicted that the corporatization of the health sector would result in the proletarianization of doctors. They argue that corporatization reduces the independence of doctors, forcing them to acquiesce to corporate control over medical decisions. In a classic article, John McKinlay and Joan Arches point out that physicians are "forced to relinquish control over the disposition of their own labor power" (1985:171). Corporatization is accompanied by bureaucratization, which brings about proletarianization and puts medical autonomy in jeopardy (Stoeckle, 1988; Derber, 1982; Starr, 1982). The process is fostered by medicine's interest in ever-increasing specialization and subspecialization, which, according to McKinlay, is deskilling in disguise (1977).

The proletarianization perspective equates the shift from an independent practice status to employee status with diminishing professionalism. But this interpretation has its detractors. Vicente Navarro, for one, argues that the medical profession was never totally responsible for shaping the organization of its work, so it cannot lose something it never had. The organization of medical practice was shaped by the fact that it evolved within a capitalist society (Navarro, 1988). Nor are doctors likely to lose complete control over their work because they will continue to possess specialized knowledge and skill that are not easily replaced (Freidson, 1986).[2]

Even if the structure of medical work is becoming more proletarianized than ever before, this may not necessarily mean that physicians themselves are becoming proletarianized. The concept "proletarian" carries certain connotations that may not apply in the case of

[2] A number of scholars argue that restructuring is not as detrimental to medical professionalism as it at first appears, since professionals who work in bureaucratic organizations are not nearly as dependent on their employers as less skilled workers (Engel, 1970; Leicht, Fennell, and Witkowski, 1995). In fact, the organizations themselves tend to take on a professional identity rather than forcing the professionals to accept the worst aspects of bureaucratic control (Engel and Hall, 1973; Bucher and Stelling, 1977).

physicians.[3] Being a member of the proletariat has traditionally meant membership in the working class. McKinlay and Arches say that proletarianization is the subordination of task activities to the "broader requirements of production under advanced capitalism" (1985:161). However, the debate that has followed has broadened this definition to address life style, values, and social status outside of the workplace. It is unlikely that physicians will become proletarianized in this sense. While that is the threat that physicians are hearing, there is little evidence that physicians who become salaried employees embrace working class values or lifestyles or have any inclination to do so. Source of income alone—salary, contractually–negotiated reimbursement rate, or fee-for-service—does not determine whether a doctor is a proletarian or deprofessionalized. As Roemer points out, the lavishly paid though salaried executives of large corporations are not proletarians; nor are street peddlers or rickshaw pullers who own their own devices necessarily any better off than workers (1986:470).

The Costs of Industrialization, Capitalism, and Bureaucracy

In the nineteenth and twentieth centuries, manufacturing evolved from a cottage industry to domination by large capitalist firms. Reviewing that transformation may help us predict whether the changes now proceeding in the health sector will have consequences for medical work comparable to the consequences that industrialization had for manufacturing work and workers. By industrialization I mean the replacement of craft work at home or in small workshops by mass machine production of goods in factories. By capitalism, I mean the form of ownership and decision-making power that operates in a market system. When I refer to the bureaucratic structures established in the process, I mean hierarchical and centralized forms of control over the work process.

Until relatively recently, the benefits of industrialization were viewed as overriding the costs. Industrialists took great pride in the

---

[3] The distinction here is between the Weberian analysis of status and prestige and the Marxist concept of class.

part they played, which they were pleased to indicate by using stationery featuring smokestacks in full operation at the top of the letterhead. They took full credit for an unprecedented achievement—the introduction of mass production techniques that enriched the quality of life by providing consumers with a vast array of affordable products. The expansion of production and jobs helped many to escape poverty. The rapid growth of industrial firms and their need for a constant supply of new workers in jobs near the bottom of the employment ladder pushed those ahead of them up the same ladder. However, industrialization, especially during its earliest stages, was brutal. Workers labored for long hours, working conditions were often dangerous, and there was no safety net for the ill or injured. Only the social reformers of the time were heard to lament such conditions.[4]

Consistent with American cultural traditions and values, the achievements of industrialization have been attributed to the capitalistic spirit of entrepreneurs. In this view, industrialists built their fortunes by applying bureaucratic principles to reduce inefficiencies. They transformed craft work into a series of low-skill tasks, moved the operation into a centralized setting—a factory—and imposed managerial control over the entire production process. High productivity was achieved at the cost of diminishing individual workers' control over the work process, in essence, by deskilling their work (Braverman, 1974).[5]

[4] The role of capitalism in industries development has been hotly debated. One aspect of the argument is disagreement over whether capitalism has had too much or too little influence on the structure of work and productivity. Those who argue that capitalism was never truly tested say that it would have brought greater benefits if its operations had not been distorted by government interference; self-regulating market forces have not been truly tested. Others view the same facts and conclude that capitalism must be tempered because it sows the seeds of its own destruction in the absence of such tempering. From this point of view, capitalism breeds social unrest by simultaneously holding out the hope of growth and improvement while generating a high level of insecurity (Martinelli and Smelser, 1990). Hence, some government intervention is necessary to maintain social order and stability.

[5] Some scholars say that the term "deskilling" misrepresents what took place, that new skills and new work opportunities were created as others fell into disuse. The evidence is mixed (Form, 1987). What is certain is that industrialization succeeded in combining the "scientific management" of Frederick Taylor with the bureaucratic organization analyzed by Max Weber (Rankin, 1990).

The process was heavily influenced by the special features of U.S. society during the nineteenth century. Workers were recruited from the ranks of poorly educated, often rural, immigrants (Attewell, 1987). They were disproportionately single men with little attachment to a community, so the labor force was far less stable than in Europe (Jacoby, 1985). The men quit without notice if they saw more opportunity elsewhere or decided they did not like what they were doing. To minimize disruption of production, foremen had to be prepared to hire new workers and put them to work the same day. These special circumstances contributed to deskilling. Control over the organization of work was shifted permanently away from individual workers to the companies that employed them. Managers and foremen were seen as critical to the vast productivity increases.

Widespread concern about the current changes in the organization of work has generated a new willingness to examine established cultural values and understandings related to work. Some scholars are asking whether industrial development could have followed a different and perhaps better route? And some answer that the route pursued was not the most rational one possible (Perrow, 1986; Edwards, 1979; White, 1992). It is in this revisionist spirit that scholars are reassessing the legacy of industrialization. Piore and Sabel (1984) argue that, since industrialization shaped the current structure of work, it is responsible for the prevailing crisis of work and workers.

From this perspective, the forces that gave birth to and nurtured the industrial revolution are played out, and the industrial model that evolved is no longer functional. Society is seen as struggling to develop a more suitable model. This is tantamount to a new phase of industrial revolution; Piore and Sabel call it "the second industrial divide." They say that the process has not come to a logical end point and therefore remains open to influence. Accordingly, this is an opportune time to test innovations. They argue for a return to craft methods of production, similar to those that existed before the first industrial divide.

Workers' Response to Industrialization

Heckscher's (1988) appraisal of the course followed by American unions is consistent with this point of view. He argues that labor organizations, which were intended to give workers a voice and permit management to deal with workers' demands in an orderly manner, have become gridlocked. Unions find it difficult to deal with problems that cannot be reduced to contractual language—which excludes virtually all the critical issues currently driving corporate sector decisions, particularly finance and technology. Workers' current situation is the direct result of the accommodations the union movement was forced to make in response to the growth of large industrial corporations in the first few decades of this century.[6]

Workers' response to industrialization is documented by labor historians in a large body of literature. Here I focus on the shift from craft unionism to industrial unionism, symbolized by the founding of the Congress of Industrial Organizations—the CIO—in 1936. The rise of the CIO, ironically, is linked to management's agenda of deskilling the workforce. The industrial union movement was a response to the rise of mass production technology and the growth of firms. As craft work was deskilled and moved into factories, workers were hired to perform low-skill tasks under the control of foremen. Craft unions, organized in the American Federation of Labor (AFL), had no way to fight this trend. They were not structured to deal with big companies, and their leaders and members, the elite of blue-collar workers, often looked down on the unskilled. Thus the CIO was founded to represent factory workers across the board, including both unskilled laborers and a smaller number of skilled tradesmen. The CIO quickly achieved bargaining power by organizing the mass industries, such as auto and steel, by firm rather than by craft.

---

[6] Much of the data on the impact of unionization on industry have appeared within the last decade or so. They indicate that unions have increased wages, but that the extent of the difference between union and non-union workers varies depending on whether the economy is in an upturn or a downturn (Gordon, Edwards, and Reich, 1982; Rubin, 1986). Whether this is interpreted as beneficial or detrimental to society's interests depends on the larger belief system of the analyst. At one end of the spectrum is the view that unions have taken advantage of industrial conditions by applying their monopolistic powers to raise wages, thereby preventing rational market forces from creating a fair market value for a worker's labor. At the other end are those who argue that unions have helped workers achieve more satisfying working conditions and that this, in turn, has fostered commitment to the firm, increased productivity, and reduced the worst social inequities (Pfeffer and Davis-Blake, 1990; Cornfield, 1991, 1989; see Freeman and Medoff, 1984, for discussion of both sides of the argument).

Much was lost with the decline of craft work (Heckscher, 1988).[7] Craft workers lost the sense of occupational community and shared interests that could be pursued not only on the job but in the hours after the job ended. The sense of belonging to an occupational community had been created and reinforced naturally as new workers learned the necessary skills from senior members of the group rather than supervisors in a firm. The sense of community plus confidence in their combined market strength helped to sustain democracy in craft unions. Attempts to create unions around occupational communities during the twentieth century have not produced lasting results. Cobble's study of waitresses in San Francisco shows the rewards of occupational community, but also why such communities find it difficult to survive in the face of corporate efforts to increase efficiency similar to those imposed during the earlier phases of industrialization (1991).

The success of the CIO has had implications for the ideology and imagery of the American labor movement ever since. The CIO's cross-industry approach united workers with different levels of skill, diverse ethnic and religious backgrounds, and differing political aspirations. What they had in common was their interest in fair treatment and fair wages. This resulted in an instrumental form of business unionism. With higher wages, families could aspire to, and attain, a lifestyle much like that enjoyed by the middle class. If unions could give their members a chance to attain the American Dream, then members had no reason to be interested in expanding the role of the union beyond business unionism (Kessler-Harris, 1987). In short, American unions were in a weak position to pursue an agenda of social or political change (Hattam, 1993). They took a more narrow approach, operating from their strength and limiting their agenda to "bread and butter issues."

[7] The style of life and work associated with craft unionism is attracting renewed interest because other idealized lifestyles no longer promise the same level of reward as in the past. For example, self-employment has long been a socially sanctioned alternative to a professional career. Some now argue that over the last few decades, it has become a mockery of the ideal of the good life (Linder, 1992). Linder provides evidence that rather than approximating the ideal of self-sufficiency and independence, "self-employment" now serves as a face-saving self-identification, to cover unintended partial employment and unemployment.

Labor law also helped to shape the union movement in this country. Early labor legislation was designed to address the issues that arose because workers were fighting for a greater share of the wealth and for improved working conditions in industrial settings. In focusing on issues relevant to that era, the law has had the effect of restricting the array of issues unions are permitted to address today. This leaves newly emerging workplace issues outside the unions' realm. Laws governing workers' rights in general and their application to physicians' unionizing efforts in particular are discussed in Chapter 13.

One of the most powerful impediments to unionization in the United States is unions' negative image, as revealed in the "confidence in social institutions" survey discussed in Chapter 5. Some scholars argue that this negative image is a legacy of the narrow business unionism the labor movement has pursued (Edwards and Podgursky, 1986; Kochan, 1979, 1985). Others maintain that the American value system holds competitive individualism, and values closely linked to capitalism, in such high regard that any effort to appeal to a stronger social orientation is unlikely to receive much support (Lipset, 1986).[8]

In short, capitalism offered a set of ideals consistent with the course of industrial development. The labor movement emerged to give voice to the workers who were swept up in this development. Industrial unionism found an avenue that allowed workers to accommodate rather than challenge the structure of work created by industrialization. Unionists argued for a bigger piece of the reward pie— not changes in work structure or future development.

As the industrial era comes to a close in this country, the structure of work is undergoing vast reorganization once again, under very different conditions. Workers are no longer prepared to move as readily in pursuit of a better job, especially now that families often include two persons whose careers must be considered. The tasks they perform do not always lend themselves as readily to deskilling;

---

[8] Lipset sees evidence for this in the revival, in the post-war boom years, of the traditionally libertarian views that had been suppressed during the New Deal 1930s. The 1980s marked the culmination of competitive individualism, which would run its course by the end of the decade (Lipset, 1986).

indeed, strict rules and job descriptions are being redefined and in many cases determined to be unnecessarily restrictive. But while these trends characterize the most technically advanced industries, health sector managers are actively pressing health care workers to accept the imposition of a traditional, bureaucratic form of work organization that depends on centralized, hierarchical control.

There are some indications, however, that medicine's transformation from cottage industry to a modern stage of production may still have a chance to be redirected—that it may not follow the same route to bureaucracy and hierarchy that manufacturing did. The shift from an industrial to a postindustrial stage of production is spurring corporate leaders to experiment with new organizational structures and controls over work. How the shift from an industrial to a postindustrial era might affect "knowledge workers" such as doctors is the topic of Chapter 12.

❧ 12 ❧

Postindustrial Work:
A New Class of Workers

Health care organizations and workers produce services, not goods. Those who advocate moving the health sector out of the cottage stage have not paid enough attention to the differences between goods-producing and service delivery enterprises. They are paying even less attention to the special circumstances of the medical profession.

While industrialization completely transformed the goods-producing sector of society, it had relatively little direct impact on the delivery of services. By comparison, the changes in the service sector have been slow and anything but uniform. Even as industrialization was achieving tremendous gains, providing consumers with an ever-increasing array of high-quality products, services remained exempt from such expectations. While goods production was being rationalized via centralization, automation, and standardization, the service sector continued to be individualized and decentralized.

Until relatively recently, the delivery of services has not been a matter of public scrutiny because the nature of and payment for services have been regarded as matters appropriately settled by the parties involved. The freedom of one person to engage another, in order to benefit from the other's special skills or simply willingness to carry out the task, is basic to the conception of the free market. Payment for professional services, in particular, was arranged between individuals without public interference in matters of cost or quality, as befits a truly free-market system. Thus there was no pressing need to rationalize the structure of service work.

Now that the industrial era is coming to a close in this country, corporations and government are shifting attention away from the goods-producing sector to the service sector. They are changing the previous *laissez faire* arrangements for the delivery of services. In fact, the rapid pace at which service work is being rationalized, centralized, bureaucratized—that is, undergoing a process very similar to industrialization—is troubling to some observers. George Ritzer captures its essence when he calls this process "McDonaldization" (1993), while Barbara Garson relates the baleful nuances in full and rich detail (1988). Thus far, services have been rationalized where standardization is considered positive and where personal involvement with the individual who produces the service is not highly regarded. Fast food customers expect the hamburger to be cooked exactly the same way each time and expect little else from fast food workers; car owners want their oil changed quickly without getting involved in discussions about buying other services; bank customers have become accustomed to teller machines available whenever they need cash.

This does not mean, however, that all services can be expected to evolve along the same lines, at least not in the foreseeable future, for four reasons. For one, the service sector is heterogeneous—it includes everything that is not goods production or agriculture. The service sector can mean everything from fast food preparation, to policing, to developing software programs, to interpreting magnetic resonance images.

Second, efforts to rationalize the service sector are being launched at a different and more complex time in history than the time when industrialization began. Although it was not directly affected by the industrial revolution, the service sector did not remain frozen during that period; it adapted to shifts in social expectations and technological applications over the last two centuries. As a result, delivery patterns, institutions, and markets evolved in the service sector and became institutionalized.

Third, the entire service sector is not about to become fully rationalized, or McDonaldized, because society is not prepared to see all services standardized and bureaucratized. While the industrial model of work organization has been successfully imposed onto some services, it is not as well suited to those society considers personal, unique, or specially matched to the client's individual preferences. Robert Reich observes that human beings have an almost insatiable desire for the personal attention provided by this sector (1991:286). Self-improvement services for the psyche or the body come to mind. We are very particular about services performed by professionals, or those that depend on a high level of technical skill.

Fourth, workers with highly specialized and sophisticated skills can resist the imposition of tighter organizational control over their work and prevent standardization. Such occupations maintain their distinctive histories and identities even when they work in large organizations (certified public accountants, chaplains in the armed forces, or physicists, for example). Their work is often governed by well-developed norms regarding interactions with clients that are formulated under the auspices of associations outside of individual work settings.[1]

Flexible Work, Flexible Workers

No one disputes that the role of the United States as a leading industrial power has peaked and is in decline, as other countries

---

[1] A puzzling trend is now well established in some segments of the service sector: traditional services have been relabeled "products." In banking, finance, insurance, and various consulting operations, firms employ account executives charged with marketing a range of "products." The technical quality of the product rather than the quality of the service is emphasized. Can it be that greater glamor is thought to be associated with goods than with services? Perhaps goods production is thought to inspire greater confidence than service delivery. Or is this a vivid illustration of traditional industrialization processes being applied in the service sector?

Is it possible that labeling financial services as "product packages" allows managers to disaggregate necessary skills, standardize the tasks involved, and deprofessionalize the account executives—in short, to deskill the workers who have been in a position to offer individualized attention to a client's investment needs? These managers present standardization of products as an effort to insure high quality with reduced risk. Since the account executives may advise their clients about a shrinking number of standardized financial packages, their education and experience become less relevant. (I am indebted to Roberta Garner for this interpretation.) As one account executive put it, she was feeling like a Fuller Brush salesperson.

I am tempted to predict that the current situation is a fleeting phenomenon, since any differentiation among "products" is bound to become less apparent as companies compete to deliver the ones customers find most attractive. This, in turn, once more turns the quality of "service" associated with the product into a marketable differentiating characteristic that firms will want to promote. Health insurance reform may provide a test of this prediction. It remains to be seen whether financial institutions conclude that it makes sense to replace better educated account executives with clerical workers.

become more industrialized. The United States has been moving
ahead into a new postindustrial phase (Touraine, 1971). The characteristics of the period were delineated by Daniel Bell over two decades ago. He identified five signposts of the postindustrial era (1973):

1) the economic sector: change from a goods-production to a
service economy

2) occupational distribution: preeminence of the professional
and technical class

3) axial principle: centrality of theoretical knowledge as the
source of innovation and of policy formation for society

4) future orientation: control of technology and technological
assessment

5) decision making: creation of a new "intellectual technology."

One of the most significant changes in the new era is the growing recognition that the work performed by postindustrial workers,
which depends on a high level of technical skill and coordination,
does not benefit from bureaucratic controls (Fligstein, 1990). Thus a
clearly articulated managerial hierarchy, detailed job descriptions,
and procedures defining tasks to be performed are seen as barriers to
organizational flexibility—impediments to the creativity that might
be released were the individuals who perform complex tasks given
more freedom.

Today's consumers are less impressed by the assurance of quality
that has traditionally characterized standardized products. They expect not only high-quality products but ones that meet their special
requirements. This means that producers of technically sophisticated
products must be willing both to adapt what they produce and to
work with the clients so that they may take full advantage of those
products. Thus we see a "new class" of workers, familiar enough with
technologically sophisticated products to help customers develop individualized applications. Such workers operate in a wide range of
enterprises and have been called intellectual laborers, knowledge
workers, or educated workers (Harrington, 1972; Mallet, 1975;
Bruce-Biggs, 1979; Gouldner, 1979; Hargrove, 1986).

The work of the new class is not easily supervised and controlled.
It is often performed by teams of specialists or passed from one group
of specialists to another. This kind of work is difficult to subdivide,
even when those in charge are themselves technically skilled. In-

deed, it is the ability of these educated workers to devise creative solutions to complex problems that cannot be subdivided that is the essence of their value to the organization. The skills they are expected to bring to their work include the ability to integrate and interpret the technical information they handle. Their continued value depends on their readiness to upgrade their skills. Employers are discovering that expecting such workers to carry out their assignments within more traditional bureaucratic structures reduces their productivity. The restrictive nature of such structures dampens workers' efforts to explore solutions by using the knowledge of persons outside their own areas of expertise, to make use of creative spurts by working unconventional hours, and to follow through on unexpected findings.

Management-Controlled Flexibility

While corporate executives are learning that it is self-defeating to impose too many rules and procedures, they are not necessarily sanguine about the implications for controlling employees' work. Accordingly, managerial efforts to divide work into discrete activities and routinize it have not been abandoned. Recognition that the new class of workers must be treated differently may not diminish corporate commitment to the industrial model of work organization wherever possible. A study of computer programming provides an illustration. Philip Kraft (1977) finds that in the managerial vision, programming teams are to be like surgical teams: a chief is assisted by persons of different and mostly lower levels of skill. This legitimates both hierarchical control over the work process, in the person of the chief programmer/manager, and the shift of a large number of tasks to workers with only vocational training.

The extent to which corporations are intentionally aiming to restrict the powers of the new class of knowledge workers, and succeeding, is difficult to determine. That U.S. corporations are becoming increasingly dependent on knowledge workers is, however, very clear. Writers on management techniques have focused on the need to improve work arrangements to enhance the productivity of the new class of workers (Kantor, 1990; Erickson, 1990). One innovation is greater reliance on work teams. It is true that the teams may be encouraged to compete with each other, and that they are headed by experts who assume some managerial functions. Nevertheless, teams are a significant reversal of the hierarchical approach to organizing work associated with the industrial era. It proceeds from the idea that supervisors are no longer necessary in postindustrial settings. Indeed, middle managers are routinely blamed for dragging down profits, laid off, or simply fired.

Another trend is the breakdown of traditional compensation arrangements linked to seniority, place in the hierarchy, and status. Corporations are said to be moving from "position to performance"; from "status to contribution"; from "bureaucracy to internal entrepreneurship" (Kantor, 1989). A growing portion of the new class has no job security at all. They enter into contractual agreements with employers with the understanding that they are there to complete a particular assignment over a specified period of time. They are not employees; they are "contract workers."

It is not clear whether such competitive arrangements will become the norm or whether workers will eventually rebel, especially if their contributions are evaluated on a short-term basis (Mallet, 1975). They may react by taking competition to the extreme, resorting to ruthless and illegal activities to gain an advantage. Some workers may tire of the instability and insecurity of such jobs and demand more stable and less competitive arrangements. Just as employers are trying to determine how to build structures that will best harness the skills of educated workers, the workers themselves are faced with working out their own occupational expectations. The extent to which they will shift from an individualistic approach to a collective approach remains to be seen. They have strong feelings about the value of the knowledge they bring to their work, as do members of the traditional professions. On the other hand, they have shown little interest in adopting the model of work and identity long embraced by the established professions.

Unlike professionals, the new class of workers do not object to being defined as employees, even temporary employees, of large organizations. Having no predecessors who carried out similar tasks outside of organizations, they have no tradition of independence from organizational constraints. Thus, neither they nor the organizations with which they are associated have shown much interest in debating whether they should be defined as professionals. Persons who analyze data of all sorts, for example, economists who work for major stock brokerage houses or biochemists in pharmaceutical corporations, all seem untroubled by the notion that employee-like status poses a threat to their autonomy, which is a central concern to those in the established professions.

In projecting the fate of postindustrial workers, Daniel Bell thought it too early to judge whether the new class would accept all the ramifications of employee status. He argued that they might still seek to define themselves as professionals, overcoming the new left rhetoric that denigrated professionalism as "elitism." But Bell predicted that such workers would ultimately develop a collective identity in the process of identifying common occupational objectives. While his prediction has not materialized over the last twenty years, his concern is worth keeping in mind: "Few groups would remain unorganized for long. . . . The major question in the next two decades will be the character of these organizations: will they retain their traditional guild form, or become more militant and aggressive labor unions?" (1973:144)

As Bell suggests, if postindustrial workers decide to challenge their employers in order to change the conditions of their work, they will have to give some thought to what kind of organizations to construct (Piore, 1985). They will have to create labor organizations that do not depend so heavily on work rules, job descriptions, seniority rules, and all the other features of work associated with industrial unionism. A number of occupational groups have been experimenting with new forms of organization in an effort to achieve exactly that. They are developing new and expanding occupational and organizational objectives, and they have designed innovative compensation arrangements that permit individuals to seek settlements separate from those negotiated by the majority within the same union. Chapter 16 includes some examples.

The UAPD represents an occupational group that has much in common with the new class of postindustrial workers, whose work combines the delivery of services with the development and application of sophisticated technical products. Its style of representation is very different from industrial unionism. In identifying the services the UAPD offers its members, we can see what it offers that is special, and what this category of the new class of workers sees as valuable enough to convince them to join a union.

❧ 13 ☙

Is It Legal for Doctors
to Form Unions?

A ccording to Dr. Marcus, anyone and everyone may join a
union, because a "union" is merely the coming together of two
or more persons for purposes of accomplishing the common good.
UAPD attorneys agree. But not all individuals do have this right
when pursuit of the common good has market effects, specifically
effects on the price of labor (Horty, 1975; Sobal and Hepner, 1990).

By law, only "employees" involved in an employee-employer relationship may engage in activities aimed at promoting their mutual
self-interest via collective bargaining over wages and working conditions. Persons who are not "employees" may not engage in collective
bargaining or any other collective action aimed at increasing their
wages or the prices of their products. This is "price-fixing," and it is
illegal.

However, as Dr. Marcus states in a March 1985 UAPD Newsletter,
the law has not prevented the UAPD from representing doctors
many of whom are not "employees."

The Union of American Physicians and Dentists (UAPD),
which has effectively represented its private practice and employed members for almost thirteen years in a perfectly legal
manner, has constantly had to defend itself against the detractors who warned that it could not do so. For all of those years,
the UAPD has acted vigorously and openly as a labor union for
doctors. . . .

The Union of American Physicians and Dentists firmly in-
tends to go right on doing what it has done so well—
representing doctors in ALL practice modes and settings—to the

best of its ability, and IN FULL CONFORMITY WITH LABOR AND
ANTI-TRUST LAW!

Dr. Marcus's assertion aside, the legal question is not so much,
"Who can join a union?" as "Who is considered an 'employee' and
therefore eligible for collective bargaining?" This chapter reviews
those arguments, without taking sides.

Labor Law and Precedents

General labor legislation addresses both workers' rights and restrictions on activities that affect the price of goods, services, and
wages. The Sherman Antitrust Act of 1890 aimed to restrict the
emergence of monopolies. It was designed to prevent interference
with interstate commerce, restraint of competition, and collusion to
increase prices. It made clear that price-fixing was subject to legal
sanction regardless of who engages in it. By not mentioning workers'
organizing efforts, the law established by exclusion, workers' rights
to organize and bargain collectively.

The Clayton Act of 1914 stated that human labor is not to be
treated as a commodity or article of commerce, and made labor organizing a legally protected right. Section four of the 1932 Norris–
LaGuardia Act prohibited court injunctions against employees engaged in actions growing out of a labor dispute. The intent of this
law was further clarified in section five, which declared that no injunction may be issued in order to prevent participation in a labor
dispute on the grounds that such action constitutes an unlawful combination or conspiracy. It is also true that the courts have been finding an increasing number of reasons to issue such injunctions in spite
of the Norris–LaGuardia legislation. In 1935, Congress passed the
National Labor Relations Act, known as the Wagner Act after its
primary author. The law was written for the express purpose of outlining employees' rights to organize in unions, bargain collectively,
and engage in concerted actions leading to improved wages and
working conditions. It created the National Labor Relations Board
(NLRB) to protect workers' efforts to form unions, hold elections
to determine the level of support for a union, and resolve labor/
management disputes via arbitration.

The Wagner Act reaffirmed the requirement that persons protected by labor law must be employees, engaged in an employee-employer relationship. It stated that the term "employee" does not include supervisors or independent contractors, and excluded public employees from NLRB jurisdiction. Later court interpretations put independent contractors in a position closer to that of independent businessmen. The law made clear, however, that professionals who are employees have the right to bargain collectively.

In determining whether the persons attempting to organize are employees, the courts have considered degree of skill, authority to hire and discharge workers, method and determination of compensation, whether the individual has an independent entrepreneurial interest in the venture, whether the tools are furnished and maintained by the employer, and whether the employer has control over the premises where the services are performed.

In *Taylor v. International Union of Horseshoers*, the courts determined that the union and its members were in violation of antitrust laws. The court found that, in spite of the fact that journeymen farriers were salaried employees, they were actually working as "independent contractors." The court determined that farriers, or horseshoers, were so highly specialized that horse trainers and horse owners could assert little control over them. Farriers provided their own tools, worked at their own pace, and took responsibility for bringing new skills to bear as needed. As a result, their effort to set prices for shoeing racehorses, and the boycott that followed, violated antitrust laws (*Taylor v. International Union of Horseshoers, Local 7*, 353 F. 2nd 593, 1965). The court held that workers who face little competition from others doing like work must be considered "independent contractors" because their position is similar to that of independent businessmen.

The courts have permitted, however, unions that include both workers in employee-employer relationships and individuals who do the same work as independent contractors. A 1940 case involved independent milk vendors who bought milk from dairies and then sold it on consignment. The court ruled that the independent drivers could belong to the same union as the salaried drivers because they were doing the same work, even though this was anti-competitive (*Milk Wagon Drivers' Union v. Lake Valley Farm Products*, 311 U.S. 91, 1940). The courts reached the same decision with regard to bakery and pastry drivers (*Bakery and Pastry Drivers and Helpers Local v. Wohl*, 317 U.S. 769, 1941) and owner-operator truckers (*Teamsters Local 24 v. Oliver*, 358 U.S. 282, 1959).

Similarly, the musicians' union was permitted to determine band leaders' charges even though the band leaders were acting as employers of other musicians. The court's reasoning was that the band leaders were using the "tools of the trade" and working as musicians during engagements. Therefore, they were entitled to benefit from the agreement reached by the musicians' union (*American Federation of Musicians v. Carroll*, 391 U.S. 99, 1968). The finding reaffirmed a 1960 case concerned with the rights of barbers who are at the same time employers and sole proprietors of barber shops (*Journeyman Barbers v. Messner*, 53 Cal. 2nd 873, 1960). The same interpretation was applied to actors in 1981 (*H.A. Artists and Associates, Inc. v. Actors' Equity Association*, 451 U.S. 704, 1981).

Employees or Independent Contractors?

Are physicians independent contractors—like farriers—under all circumstances, and therefore not eligible for protection under labor law? This question is addressed in the medical press each time a new group of physicians tests the question in the courts. Determining whether doctors can collectively bargain over fees and/or salaries is of concern to both doctors and the organizations in which they work (Strand and Mickelsen, 1990; Maressa, 1986).

In 1993 the AMA asked doctors whether they considered themselves employees or independent contractors. The survey found that 31.1 percent considered themselves employees (Oberman, 1994). That number has been steadily increasing, while the number who define themselves as independent contractors (4.8%) or self-employed (64.1%) has been declining.

Calling oneself an employee is not, however, enough to qualify for protection under labor law. UAPD staff members, among others, argue that physicians are now in a situation much like that faced by the vast majority of workers prior to the emergence of unions. Workers were told what wage the employer was prepared to offer; they had the option of taking it or leaving it. In this view, physicians are in the same position vis-à-vis third-party payers. A document circulated by the Illinois Physicians Union in the mid-1970s argued that the precedent for determining the eligibility of physicians could be found in *NLRB v. Hearst Publications*, 322 U.S. 111 (1944): "News-boys . . . have their wages influenced in large measure by the publishers, who dictate their buying and selling prices, fix their markets and control their supply of papers. Their hours of work and their efforts are supervised and to some extent prescribed by the publishers or their agents" (Baffes, 1974).

Or, as Dr. Marcus has noted more recently, it is not clear why doctors should be excluded when so many other occupational groups whose employee status is not any more clearly established are allowed to bargain collectively.

> We can cite ad infinitum such examples as professional baseball and football players, journeymen barbers, musicians, motion picture actors and directors, owner-operators of Teamster trucks, and a host of others; none of whom are any more "sala-, ried" workers than we are, but have been granted the legal right to form unions of their own, to engage in true collective bargaining on economic issues and, most important, to enjoy the applicable exclusions from anti-trust laws that are uniquely granted to bona-fide trade unions but which are withheld from professional associations. It is amusing but true that the motion picture producers, hardly an economically downtrodden or impoverished group, have now formed a trade union of their own, under the Teamsters, of all things! (1986a:22)

The AMA, on the other hand, argues that physicians have traditionally been considered independent contractors and that the changes in the health care system, as disadvantageous as they may be, do not alter physicians' status under the law (1984). Physicians continue to be independent contractors no matter what kind of contractual payment arrangements they enter into. A Board of Trustees report acknowledges that third-party payers and hospitals "have seized a substantial measure of economic control over the physicians' practice" (1984:9). However, "control over the mode and manner of the performance of medical services remains with the physician" (1984:9); physicians have control over their work by virtue of their

professional autonomy which is protected from interference by statutory medical practice acts. The AMA view is that the NLRB and
the federal courts "undoubtedly would consider the physician's wide
discretion in the exercise of professional skill and judgment particularly persuasive evidence of independent contractor status" (1984:9)

The AMA has not changed its position since the early 1970s,
when the sudden interest in unionization among physicians across
the country caused it to do a historical review. A document produced
by the AMA legal department in 1972 included the following examples:

1941—the Kings County Physicians Guild, which included 700
    members as of 1966.
1956—the Nassau Physicians' Guild; 1,000 members as of 1966.
1961—the Staten Island Physicians' Guild; 110 members in 1966.
1966—the United Physicians Association, incorporated in Florida;
    1,000 members as of 1972.
1972—the Nevada Physicians Union, Local 676, an affiliate of the
    Service Employees International Union, AFL-CIO.

But the AMA Board concluded that unions'

> traditional emphasis on collective action through strict major-
> ity rule is ill-suited to professional values of individualism and
> autonomy. Organizationally and philosophically, moreover,
> the labor union model comprehends neither of the pursuits that
> are of paramount importance to physicians organized in profes-
> sional associations—the advancement of medical science and
> the promotion of public and patient welfare. (Report F, quoted
> in AMA Board of Trustees Report L, 1984)

When the Board reviewed the issue in 1984, it reaffirmed its
earlier stance, stating, "Legal and socio-economic developments have
made unionization a more attractive yet less realistic option for the
vast majority of physicians."

Salaried Physicians

It seems logical to expect that physicians who work on a salaried
basis for a single organization, rather than contracting with one or

more organizations, would be considered employees and eligible for protection under labor law. Interestingly, the AMA document of 1984 acknowledges that a small proportion of physicians are truly engaged in bona fide employee-employer relationships and agrees that they should be able to bargain collectively.

Not long after the AMA Trustees issued this report, the National Labor Relations Board determined that physicians employed by hospitals could be represented by a newly approved union that would bargain collectively on behalf of all hospital employees (Rosman, 1975). The decision did not produce a lasting solution, however, since physicians were not willing to join bargaining units that included unskilled hospital workers.

While the number of salaried physicians continues to increase, the question of whether they have the right to bargain has not been as firmly established as the unions representing them would like. In 1985, the UAPD lost its bid to represent a group of doctors employed by the Family Health Plan HMO in southern California. The employer argued that they were management employees (*UAPD Newsletter*, October 1985). The court agreed, determining that the doctors were persons who "formulate and effectuate management policies" and "represent management interest by taking or recommending actions that effectively control or implement employer policy" (McCracken, 1986:11).

Dr. Marcus took the position that the decision was only a temporary setback to the physicians' union movement. He maintained that the ruling applied to that particular HMO and did not mean that the courts would issue a similar ruling in other cases. The experience of the Doctors' Council of New York bore him out (Trubo, 1989). The court ruled that 105 doctors working full-time at Coney Island Hospital could not bargain collectively because they had managerial status. However, it did permit 86 doctors who worked less than three-quarters time at the hospital to organize. The 86 doctors selected the Council to represent them by a two-to-one margin.

One of the main obstacles to collective bargaining for salaried physicians is the *NLRB v. Yeshiva University* decision (444 U.S. 672, 1980). In that case, the court decreed that university faculty members play a managerial role when they sit on committees charged with setting organizational guidelines and policies that have a direct effect on organizational governance; for this reason, they may not join together for collective bargaining because such action is contrary to the interests of the employer.

The reasoning behind the *Yeshiva* decision is worth examining more closely. The minority opinion presented in *NLRB v. Health Care and Retirement Corporation of America* (114 S. Ct. 1771, 1994) offers a thorough critique. The value of this critique is that it identifies points which can serve as a foundation for arguments favoring organizing rights in subsequent cases; and, as those who support the UAPD repeatedly say, there is every reason to believe the law will shift to allow physician unionism. The case takes up the question of whether nurses in supervisory positions have the right to bargain collectively. The NLRB found that nurses were not supervisors under the NLRA and ordered the nurses reinstated. In reviewing the decision, the U.S. Supreme Court upheld the decision of the Court of Appeals which reversed the NLRB's decision. Although the case concerns nurses, the same issues apply to physicians.

The minority opinion states that the majority did not give sufficient attention to the fact that the nature of professionals' work responsibilities means that they must on occasion direct and supervise the work of others (SCR, 1994:1786).

> Section 2(12) [of the NLRA] defines "professional employee" as one whose work is "predominantly intellectual and varied in character," involves "the consistent exercise of discretion and judgment in its performance," produces a result that "cannot be standardized in relation to a given period of time," and requires knowledge "in a field of science or learning customarily acquired by a prolonged course of specialized intellectual instruction and study in an institution of higher learning or a hospital." (SCR, 1994:1786)[1]

The minority concludes that the reasoning in the *Yeshiva* case as it is applied in this case creates a false dichotomy (SCR, 1994:1782).

[1] The decision in *NLRB v. Health Care and Retirement Corp.* (114 S.Ct. 1778, 1994) and dissenting opinion is found in the 114 *Supreme Court Reporter*, 1994, pages 1778–1793. In referencing specific pages, I refer to it as SCR, 1994.

In this instance "acts taken in connection with patient care and acts taken in the interest of the employer" are necessarily the same (SCR, 1994:1782). The court's reasoning in the *Yeshiva* case was that the faculty's interests and the interests of the institution are "distinct, separable entities" (SCR, 1994:1782). However, the Court of Appeals more accurately held that, "The 'business' of a university is education." The interests cannot be separated.

In the estimation of the minority, the heavy reliance on the *Yeshiva* approach is "puzzling." The intent of the NLRA was to insure that supervisory personnel could not organize against the interests of the employer. The employer was held to be "entitled to the undivided loyalty" of its managerial staff (SCR, 1994:1792). In health care organizations, however, patient care is the business of the employer comparable to education and universities. Therefore, the work performed by professionals, even when the tasks overlap into supervisory activities, is in the employer's interests.

While physicians' eligibility for protection under the NLRA continues to be unsettled, the proponents of physicians' unions are far from discouraged. They argue that persistence pays off, pointing out that many of the most effective unions—in printing, construction, and the maritime trades, for example—came into existence before the NLRA. Relying on the Board is a mistake in any case because it is administratively slow, tends to be influenced by the politics of the party in power, and is reluctant to use all the powers granted to it by Congress (McCraken, 1986).

Additionally, since states have the authority to override federal antitrust laws under specified conditions, it is more useful to seek exemption from federal restrictions on organizing at the state level. The states may permit negotiations between designated units or parties that would otherwise be prohibited by federal antitrust laws, in the interest of increased efficiency. California passed such a law in 1981, which allowed the UAPD to bargain collectively with state and local government agencies employing doctors.

One state is pursuing an approach that promises to set a precedent for doctors' bargaining rights. Over the last few years, Vermont has attempted to implement a landmark reform law that would create a single health care authority mandated to operate within a binding global budget. The state medical society agreed to support the legislation on the condition that it be granted collective bargaining rights (Meyer, 1993b). The legislation passed but, but funding continued to be a stumbling block. Because the reform would affect the state's Medicaid program, the plan had to be approved by the Health Care Financing Administration. The plan received approval in mid-1995 to begin January 1996 (U.S. General Accounting Office, 1995:75). The fact that Vermont doctors held out for collective bargaining rights in exchange for supporting the legislation must be viewed as a signal event.

Other Organizing Options

At about the same time that the physicians' union movement first appeared, a variety of other approaches aimed at gaining greater voice were being promoted. An idea that attracted interest for a short period was turning the medical staff organizations already present in hospitals into unions.

One proponent of such a plan argued that doctors were de facto employees of the hospital by virtue of medical staff bylaws, rules and regulations required by the Joint Commission on Accreditation of Hospitals (Blackman, 1973). Dr. Norman Blackman, the physician who promoted this idea argued that since hospital guidelines spell out the conditions of physicians' employment by specifying duties and obligations, physicians cannot act independently of such rules. They perform in the capacity of employees. That attending staff receive no wages does not mean they are not employees, because compensation does not have to be in the form of money. Compensation is any valuable consideration given for services rendered. Access to special equipment and facilities vital for a physician to practice is sufficient quid pro quo. This solution for gaining greater voice did not attract much of a following and had to be abandoned.

A small number of physicians affiliated with the Illinois Physicians Union in the mid-1970s argued for yet another approach, that medical staffs incorporate themselves. A medical staff would then be in a position to enter into contractual arrangements with the hospital board and to do so as an equal. This approach also failed to attract many proponents. It surely would not have survived a court test, given the courts' decisions over the following decade regarding the legality of independent contractors' organizing for the purpose of setting prices. The successful case brought by chiropractors against the AMA confirmed the fact that the court would not permit doctors to engage in behavior that would restrict competition, especially as it affects hospital privileges (*Wilk v. American Medical Association*, 719 F.2d 207, 1983).

The courts have been consistent in their determinations that physicians' attempts to engage in fee-setting are tantamount to price-fixing. *Arizona v. Maricopa County Medical Society* (457 U.S. 332, 1982) determined that physicians were engaging in illegal price-fixing by attempting to establish a maximum fee schedule using "relative value scales" together with a conversion factor. It is interesting to find, therefore, that a version of that formula, the Resource Based Relative Value Scale (RBRVS) (Hsiao, 1988), was adopted nationally by the Health Care Financing Administration in 1992. It was introduced to regulate the fees of physicians participating in Medicare. This turn of events lends support to proponents of physician unionization who say that the law is an organic, changing entity.

The Right of House Staff to Organize

Residents and interns seeking to organize were discouraged by a 1976 NLRB decision. The Board found these physicians-in-training, or house officers, to be students, not employees. Accordingly, the Physicians National House Staff Association (PNHSA), which was seeking recognition as a national union, was ineligible for NLRB protection (Andrews, 1978).

Because the NLRB has no authority over public sector organizations and workers, the ruling did not prevent residents in public hospitals from organizing, though their peers in private hospitals were prohibited from doing so. The residents in public hospitals also received a great deal of support for their activities from the Federal Labor Relations Authority, an agency created in 1979 to govern union activities among federal workers throughout the country. The agency first extended organizing rights to residents in the Veterans Administration hospitals in Los Angeles in 1982 and in Brooklyn the following year ("Housestaff . . . ," 1982:10). This helped launch the Committee of Interns and Residents (CIR) which in 1990 reported a membership of 5,000 affiliated with hospitals in New York City, New Jersey, and Washington, D.C. (Page, 1990:33). Organizing successes in other parts of the country have come in fits and starts during the 1980s. By 1990, however, the California Association of Interns and Residents was able to report that it had a membership of 1,000 and had voted to affiliate with the Service Employees International Union (SEIU) (Page, 1990:1). In 1993, the 500-member House Staff Association of Cook County Hospital in Chicago joined the American Federation of State, County, and Municipal Employees (AFSCME) ("Physicians Join Union," 1993).

The efforts of house staff to unionize caused considerable controversy within the medical establishment (Relman, 1979). The movement also attracted the attention of researchers, who explored charges that the movement signaled deprofessionalization and an impending decline in the quality of care. Gloria Engel and her colleagues (1979) surveyed house staff members of a large medical center in 1973 and 1976 to identify the characteristics of those who favored unionization. Respondents who espoused high patient care ideals also had more favorable attitudes toward unionization, particularly if they had fathers who were members of a profession. The researchers concluded that the "union might be seen as an appropriate tool for achieving patient care by those whose class status is not threatened by a working-class symbol" (1979:351); indeed, it might well be viewed "as a tool for achieving professional aims" (1979:352).

Collective Bargaining versus Unionization

Although the AMA has not altered its view of physicians' unions, it has been moving over the last few years toward adopting a far more positive stance on collective bargaining (Meyer, 1989a). It now argues that collective bargaining is an acceptable professional mechanism for interacting with the government and other third-party payers (McCormick, 1993c). Whether this is a response to changing attitudes of its members or an independent recognition of the new realities physicians face is not clear. The AMA's newsletter put it this way:

Does collective physician action on fiscal and regulatory issues have a future outside the rubric of major health reform?

Organized medicine, seeking authority for such moves as a sign of "professionalism," thinks it does. . . .

"Collective activity" can take many forms. It is most often associated with the heavy-handed collective bargaining that is the stock of trade unions, with strike threats as the union's ultimate trump card.

But proponents of a collective negotiating role for physicians with the buyers of health care envision a more genteel approach (McCormick, 1992:3).

On the position taken by doctors in Vermont, the newsletter commented: "The AMA doesn't like the global budgeting aspect of the Vermont plan. . . . But the agreement to recognize a negotiating role for medicine is dear to the Association's heart" (McCormick, 1992, 44).

It is also possible that physicians are being swayed by the views of important medical establishment representatives such as Arnold Relman, former editor of the *New England Journal of Medicine.* In Relman's view, the expansion of "managed competition" will force physicians to enter into arrangements with competing managed care organizations. He warns that corporate managers are primarily interested in responding to consumer demand, and that physicians must resist pressure to succumb to such a superficial objective and strive instead to maintain professional independence in making patient care decisions. (Because consumers are not in a position to judge what is competent care, using consumer demand as a criterion may lead to inappropriate action.)

Relman takes the position that under such conditions the best approach is strengthening professionalism through collective organization and collective bargaining. He acknowledges that current antitrust laws prohibit physicians from bargaining collectively. He notes that the national debate over health care reform that began in 1992 recognized this problem, and hopes this debate will eventually produce a more "even playing field," in which the health insurance industry loses its antitrust exemption and physicians gain the right to bargain collectively (1993).

In the end, it is interesting to compare the arguments and options presented by representatives of the medical establishment, such as Dr. Relman, to those advocated by Dr. Marcus. Dr. Relman's comments seem to be entirely consistent with Dr. Marcus's admonition:

> Either you'll sell out to management, and become part of the mechanism that oppresses and exploits your colleagues, or you'll stand together with other worker doctors. . . . Physicians cling to this entrepreneurial, go-it-alone thing out of pure nostalgia and vanity. (Bumke, 1987:65)

❧ 14 ☙

What Does the UAPD Do
for Its Members?

W hat Dr. Marcus said he wanted to achieve through the
UAPD was fair treatment for doctors.

> Now I am not, under any sense, representing doctors as being
> a downtrodden minority. . . . [O]ur union represents doctors
> who have been denied due-process rights that are customarily
> granted to ax murderers: the right to be advised of the charges
> against them in advance of a kangaroo court; the right to be
> represented by an attorney; the right to cross-examine their
> accusers. . . . (Garfinkel, 1989 reprint, no page)

According to Dr. Weinmann, doctors join the UAPD because
"physicians are losing control over their practices, their lives, and
professional well-being. A lot of doctors say that they wouldn't join
us while they can see a cure. When it is the last thing that will save
them, they join so fast that your head spins."

UAPD staff members say they do not have time to stalk new
recruits. Interested doctors call because they've heard about the
union from their colleagues, or doctors at a particular hospital will
call to ask the union to make a presentation. Dr. Weinmann and a
union representative make the presentation, show a video, and answer questions. The doctors usually request a second presentation to
ask more questions, and the process continues until the doctors make
the decision to join as a group or as individuals.

The UAPD has something of a "free rider" problem. The leadership is willing to accept this cost when the benefits of its activities
accrue to the entire collectivity of doctors. The union discourages

"free ridership" when the benefits accrue to an individual who seeks to join the union after he or she is facing work-related problems. Dr. Weinmann says, "They are told that preexisting problems are not covered when they join. It's not that we tell them they can't join— but they can't bring $10,000 worth of problems in for their first $400 worth of dues." Gary Robinson notes that the union would not, for example, help out a doctor who came to the UAPD only *after* he'd been fired.

Two Types of Membership

In a 1979 letter to members, Dr. Marcus outlined the services the UAPD could offer doctors. The union had developed the single largest repository of information about HMOs, workers' compensation, doctors' negotiating rights, doctor-hospital contract negotiations, coping with government inspections, due process rights of doctors, the institutional practice of medicine, collecting from recalcitrant insurance carriers, and medical legislative matters (Letter, February 15, 1979). The UAPD's expertise in any one of these areas was enough reason for a physician to consider joining. In future years the union was able to add to its knowledge and experience base without altering this framework. The union could tailor its advice to members in response to new directives and challenges as they appeared because it had been following the workings of the organizations initiating them all along.

The kinds of assistance and expertise a physician can use depends on whether he or she is salaried or in private practice. From the beginning, the union recognized that it was serving two very different populations. According to Gary Robinson, it took a few more years to learn that the two groups should receive separate newsletters. Until that time doctors in both categories would grumble that the union was doing more for the other group.

The main difference in the ways the union represents the two groups is the collective bargaining agreement. The union represents its salaried physicians by negotiating a contract with the organization that employs them. The union identifies the doctors' collective concerns and works to resolve differences with the management representatives who sit on the other side of the table.

For private practice doctors, there is no one organization with which the union negotiates; nor is there one particular set of concerns that the union might address. Doctors negotiate with managed care companies (usually more than one), hospitals and the organizations they spin off, and joint venture organizations. The new entities might include hospices, home care agencies, and durable equipment companies. Doctors find that they may have to negotiate new contracts every time one of these entities is reorganized. Depending on the circumstances, they may negotiate as individuals, part owners of a group practice, or members of a hospital staff. Doctors complain more bitterly about the increasing need to negotiate over particular treatment decisions. These negotiations may involve any of the above in addition to peer review organizations, Medicare carriers, Medicaid agencies, and private insurance companies.

Typically, the organizations with which the doctors interact as individuals do not consult with them before issuing rules and regulations that have a direct impact on the doctors' work. If the doctors are displeased, they have no mechanisms for identifying the rules and procedures they consider to be problematic. Eventually, of course, the problems are revealed by being repeatedly cited. By then they have caused considerable frustration and resentment.

The union employs techniques that are not so different from a grievance process in taking individual doctors' complaints to the organization involved. The union often uses the rules the organization itself has developed to cover its relationships with doctors, or it uses the contract the individual doctor has signed with the organization. The issues that are generally covered by contract specify the administrative procedures that must be employed in order to decrease practice privileges (the types of procedures a doctors is permitted to carry out in that particular hospital), change reimbursement arrangements, or resolve disputes regarding how much care a patient can receive. The union representative's role is much like that of an attorney or management consultant. The representatives bring a level of experience and sophistication to the process that few health sector administrators have encountered in their dealings with physicians in the past. Indeed, the union often brings more experience to the process than the administrators do. Because the health sector is changing so rapidly, the union is likely to become a party to troublesome interactions at an early stage, in many cases before the leaders on the opposite side of the bargaining table have dealt with the issue at hand.

From Collective Begging to Collective Bargaining

Let us look more closely at what the union does for its salaried members. Dr. Marcus recalls one of the union's earliest accomplishments on their behalf.

> When we started, doctors who were employed by the state were represented by a health care workers' union. The president of the union was a tough, pipe-smoking person—a tough, pipe-smoking female person. She was a licensed practical nurse. Every grievance had to be funneled through her. The union was very grudging in dealing with doctors' grievances. The union was totally unable to address their grievances. They were engaged in collective begging, not collective bargaining.
>
> These physicians had to have continuing education by state law, but they didn't get time off; they had to pay their own tuition. We brought back fairness to the position.

The UAPD had been involved in representing salaried doctors from the beginning, by appearing before committees of county boards. But the union's 1981 victory in its court fight with the state of California was the turning point in its ability to represent its members. The California Supreme Court approved collective bargaining for state-employed physicians in a 4-2 decision.

On May 11, 1981, salaried physicians voted to elect bargaining representatives ("Collective Bargaining . . . ," 1981;19). Of the 564 physicians who voted (out of a total of 1,000 employed by the state), 427 voted in favor of the UAPD (*UAPD Newsletter*, August 1981). Early the next year, the health service physicians employed on the sixteen campuses of the University of California voted on representation: 83 for the UAPD, 3 for the American Federation of Teachers, and 17 for no representation (*UAPD Newsletter*, March 1982).

Since the 1981 decision, the union has succeeded in organizing doctors working in every government-supported institution in the state except the academic physicians affiliated with the University of California system of colleges and universities.[1] They are organized into 15 separate bargaining units; the largest includes 1,250 doctors employed by the state. The other units include doctors employed by eight counties in the state and by several private clinics. The bargaining units are structured as locals under a strong steward system. The stewards are elected but receive their official appointment from the union.

The union uses a traditional bargaining approach to achieve improvements in wages and benefits. The doctors work under conditions outlined in the contract, which is usually negotiated for a two-year period, and they rely on a grievance procedure to resolve disputes with management. The union negotiates over the full range of bargaining issues beginning with salary and benefits but going on to the special topics that doctors want addressed. These include understandings governing issues such as medical staff privileges, peer review, and the handling of malpractice suits. That the number of topics covered by contracts is extensive is confirmed by their length. According to Robinson, the most recently negotiated contract in 1996 runs 74 pages with a 5-page index.

Staff representatives also help individual salaried doctors in more informal ways. One staffer gave the example of a member who was told she would have fewer vacation days than she thought she was entitled to. Rather than going to the administration of her institution, she asked the union representative to help her straighten out the problem. The doctor said she got along fine with the administration; she certainly did not want to treat this as a grievance matter. Yet she felt uncomfortable going to the administration herself to talk about it. The representative straightened out the matter during a brief visit with the administrator.

The same organizer says that in another case, the administrator of a large facility called her and said he knew that the union local would be holding a meeting that afternoon. He wanted her to call him after the meeting to tell him what the doctors' concerns were, because the doctors would be more forthright with her. She was

---

[1] According to Gary Robinson, the union has nothing to offer them since reimbursement is so heavily dependent on research funding.

pleased that both the doctors and the administration had enough confidence in her judgment to work out this kind of communication problem.

Some individual cases demand a great deal of personal attention but do not lead to satisfactory resolutions. In one case, a doctor got a bad performance review. He called the union representative, upset. He blamed the nurses for his poor evaluation and said he was preparing to take them to court. This was a doctor about whom other physicians had complained to the representative in the past. Nevertheless, she tried to help by giving him materials on how one should respond to performance evaluations. She discussed the evaluation with him, offered advice on how to change aspects of his interaction with colleagues and the nurses, and generally calmed him. She did not expect this to be the last time she would hear about his problems.

In another case, the UAPD defended and succeeded in having reinstated a doctor who was dismissed because he had an obnoxious personality. The union made the point that privileges can be withdrawn only when poor patient care can be established. In this case, the quality of patient care was not being questioned; the dismissal was therefore arbitrary (Bulletin of UAPD Local 7402, August 1981).

More typical are the cases of physicians fired because they would not compromise care to save money. One case that received attention in the UAPD's newsletter involved a doctor who was also an officer of the UAPD. When he was fired from the position of director of the Respiratory Care Service, he sued the hospital alleging that his dismissal resulted from his refusal to compromise patient care. It took three years for the case to come before the State Appellate Court. The three-judge panel found that the doctor was not afforded a hearing as provided by the staff bylaws. He was permitted to amend his legal complaint and proceed to trial. This decision sparked a response from the California Hospital Association, which encouraged its members to revise their contracts with physicians to enable administrators to bypass the medical staff in firing physicians (UAPD Newsletter, October 16, 1984).

One staff member who negotiates on behalf of salaried doctors finds an irony in the different treatment doctors receive in various settings. In her experience, public sector organizations that employ doctors and pay them a straight salary tend to be more responsive to the doctors' status than the newer, private sector organizations that are now entering into contracts with private practice doctors. She rarely has any difficulty getting public sector administrators to respond to doctors' concerns: "This is a high-status occupation; no one ever says no to a request to discuss a problem one of the doctors may be having." Private sector organizations are not always so accommodating.

That the person to whom the administrators are "not saying no" is the union staffer, not the doctor, is noteworthy. Union staff become reasonably well acquainted with administrators because they spend a fair amount of time intervening on behalf of members. Developing a relationship grounded in mutual respect is important because it permits the staffer to contact administrators directly to resolve problems.

Representing Private Practice Doctors

Dr. Marcus says that people were always telling him it was illegal for physicians in private practice to organize. His response was: "They said that about everybody!" Gary Robinson makes a similar point: "We represent private practice doctors the way that unions used to represent public employees before there was collective bargaining. You figure out what the law says; you figure out what you can do for them, then you go out and tell them—you've got to join us because we're the only people who are doing this."

Doctors in private practice join the union as individuals. They are generally not organized into locals. The exception is the local in San Jose, which Dr. Weinmann headed before he became the president of the union. However, in 1993 the union created a new structure, an Independent Practice Association (IPA) (*UAPD Newsletter*, July 1993). IPAs allow physicians to join together in order to contract with managed care organizations. The union negotiates the terms of these contracts on behalf of the IPA.

Because the union offers a such a wide range of services to its private practice members and has no scheduled time for focusing on any particular set of concerns, the union periodically surveys the membership. The last time the union carried out a survey was in 1987; 523 responses were returned. The survey listed ten issues the union regularly addresses and asked the members' top three priorities. They were:

1. Defending private practice medicine (27 percent)
2. Building a strong legislative program in Sacramento (14 percent)
3. Defending the due process rights of doctors (12 percent).

Fewer than 10 percent of the respondents listed the remaining factors as one of the top three. In declining importance these were: helping members negotiate contracts with PPOs, insurance companies and capitated plans; developing a lobbying presence in Washington, D.C.; malpractice issues; filing lawsuits on crucial issues; providing assistance and advice to members on individual problems; providing information to doctors concerning threats to medicine; and helping to strengthen medical staffs. Members who have specific problems call the union headquarters directly. Staff members all agree that the union is growing. It is attracting members from neighboring states. However, the union does not publish membership figures or official trend data. A 1995 estimate put the membership at approximately 5,000 (Mangan, 1995:119), which is considerably lower than Dr. Marcus's 1992 estimate of 30,000. Like other voluntary associations, the UAPD uses membership growth as a gross indicator of membership satisfaction.

The most direct form of assistance the union offers doctors in private practice is helping them get reimbursement they were denied by a third-party payer. Dr. Weinmann comments on the need for this form of assistance:

> For example, it could be that a patient shows up in the emergency room, you're called, you go see the patient, you submit your bill and it is denied. It is denied because of the contract the patient signed with *that* company and that you signed with *that* company. You agreed to peer review and the peer review was done, and they decided that it really wasn't an emergency. Meanwhile, you were there from midnight to 2 a.m. It wasn't really an emergency so you eat it.

The grievance department, later reorganized into the practice management department, specializes in dealing with such problems. The department's efforts can make a significant difference in a doctor's income. At another level, the level of principle, the union helps doctors collect compensation for work that was performed in good faith. Dr. Marcus believes that being denied fees to which they are entitled is one of the basic reasons for doctors' growing frustration. An example of the kinds of aggravation the practice management department deals with: One doctor's Medi-Cal claim for delivering a baby was denied because, according to the state's records, the mother was erroneously classified—as a male. The computerized system simply kept refusing the claim. It took the union three years to get the doctor's claim paid.

Doctors complain that their calls are not returned by third-party payers, computer breakdowns cause problems that take a lot of time and effort straighten out, especially with Medi-Cal, and the appeal process is a disaster because the funds to support it have been so severely cut. According to one staff member, when everything works fine, having a computerized system makes sense. When things go wrong, "you have to go back to paper," and then problems are more likely.

Dr. Weinmann notes that doctors who get help from the union on reimbursement sometimes recoup enough to renew their membership (currently $450 annually) for the following year. In the case of surgeons, the amount recovered may equal dues for the following several years. He says such an experience alone makes it obvious why doctors would renew their membership and why they would tell their colleagues about the advantages of belonging.

Another form of assistance the union provides is advice on entering into contracts with hospitals and pre-paid practice organizations. As early as 1980, the union had sufficient experience to develop an 18-page list of points for doctors to check before signing a contract. The objective was to protect physicians' due process rights.

An article in *American Medical News* illustrated the value of a well-written contract ("Radiologists . . . ," 1980). The head of a radiology department in Annapolis was unable to reach an agreement with the five radiologists in his department. He allowed their contracts to expire. As a result, the five radiologists lost their privileges without benefit of a hearing. The department head went on to hire three new radiologists with the approval of the hospital but against the wishes of the medical staff. The medical staff by a vote of 104 to 5 requested that the hospital board reconsider withdrawal of privileges. The department head prevailed because the radiologists had no contractual basis on which to base their protest.[2]

When a group of physicians develops a satisfactory solution to a problem that other doctors are likely to confront, the UAPD reports that solution to the entire membership. Thus, when one local created an especially well-thought-out revision of medical staff bylaws, the UAPD made the document available to all members (*UAPD Newsletter*, April 30, 1980).

Similarly, in 1992 California passed legislation requiring every employer, no matter how small, to develop a safety program. The union designed a program which doctors could implement in their offices. Gary Robinson says that as soon as the legislation was enacted, vendors were selling similar programs for anywhere from $300 to $4000. The California Medical Association put together a seminar for three or four hundred dollars, and the AMA published a $700 booklet. The union provided the same thing to members free. Robinson was planning similar help for members on complying with the federal Americans with Disabilities Act.

Union representatives sometimes offer advice to doctors in the initial stages of forming a practice group. The union can then help them negotiate a contract with a hospital or HMO. One staffer notes that it is difficult to convince doctors to accept the economic inte-

---

[2] Disputes about staff privileges began to attract greater attention as health sector organizations increased in size and became more competitive. In 1980 the AMA newsletter outlined the efforts of Donald Morrison, an attorney who was urging the American Bar Association to draft model legislation to guarantee due process for physicians, to cover exactly such cases as the radiologists'. The consensus at the annual meeting of the Bar Association was that statutory and case law to protect physicians' hospital privileges was still in its infancy. According to Morrison, state law to redress the damages that result from disciplinary proceedings was also unsatisfactory.

The ABA responded by organizing a mock disciplinary hearing showing how professional rivalry, financial competition, and even personality clashes could influence the outcome of disputes over privileges. The AMA newsletter did not dispute this portrayal. The number of cases coming before the courts has increased exponentially since then; a substantial body of case law now exists.

gration of their practices. As more doctors recognize that they will no longer be able to avoid it, they come to the union for advice. He tells them, when the hospital or the HMO wants to put you together, you're part of the company. When we put you together, you're independent.

Of course, the union cannot help doctors in private practice with every individual problem. Gary Robinson recalls the doctor who was charged with sexual harassment by one of his employees. After listening to the doctor's view of the situation, Robinson explained that the language the doctor was using was getting him in trouble. Calling employees "Honey" and "Sweetie" was just not appropriate. The doctor found it difficult to understand—why would that be a problem? After all, he argued, he was not at all interested in having a sexual relationship with these employees. Robinson says this man had somehow missed all the changes that have taken place in response to the women's liberation movement over the last twenty years. He didn't think the doctor could change his behavior short of some kind of intensive resocialization, which the union was not prepared to take on.

ง 15 ฅ

A Physicians' Union—
Harbinger or Anomaly?

This chapter summarizes my answers to the three over-arching questions about doctors' unions that were outlined in the introduction and then poses another: Is the UAPD a model that doctors and members of other professions or white collar occupations are likely to follow?

Question One: Why Did the UAPD Survive While Other Physicians' Unions Did Not?

It is clear that Dr. Marcus's charismatic leadership made the emergence of the UAPD possible. Because few organizations survive their charismatic leaders, the steps this particular charismatic leader took to establish a lasting organization take on greater significance. At the height of the physicians' union movement in the early 1970s, many doctors were ready to join unions; keeping them involved after this initial period of social turmoil was far more challenging. Yet the UAPD not only survived but became stronger. What makes this especially remarkable is that the UAPD succeeded while proceeding along an uncharted organizational path.

Dr. Marcus sought help charting this path. He turned first to the medical establishment, but was rebuffed. He then turned to the labor establishment, and was again rebuffed. He knew that the UAPD would benefit from being extended a degree of legitimacy by the establishment in either camp. The concept social scientists use to describe this phenomenon is "isomorphism." In both cases, Dr. Marcus was told to go be isomorphic with someone else.

Thus the UAPD was in the position of having to create itself without the benefit of organizational guidance or support. It is true that Dr. Marcus turned to experienced labor organizers to help build the UAPD. However, doctors' issues were different from those the labor organizers knew as concerns of workers in other sectors. Union organizers and leaders began by addressing only the most pressing issues, and expanded the number of issues they took on as the union increased its resources. Along the way, the union developed expertise not easily obtained elsewhere, and a reputation for using that expertise to good advantage.

The UAPD faced roadblocks thrown in its path by the California Medical Association, competing unions, and government agencies that found reasons to investigate the UAPD's operations. The fact that the health sector was undergoing unprecedented changes during this time meant that the UAPD had to adjust its focus to address a constantly changing set of problems.

The union managed to overcome another far less tangible, but crucial, obstacle—the accusation that it was unprofessional. In the past, doctors benefited by establishing a strong link between solo, fee-for-service practice and medical professionalism. Now that so many doctors work in groups, within the confines of contractually defined reimbursement arrangements, the old definition of professionalism is no longer in line with reality. The UAPD's special achievement was to convince doctors that joining this physicians' union would not compromise their professionalism, no matter what form of practice they pursued. Indeed, it has been able to convince increasing number of physicians that UAPD membership would enhance their professionalism.

The UAPD started out looking very much like other doctors' unions that did not survive. It survived because it managed to evolve from being one kind of entity—born out of frustration and swept along by the force of a larger social movement—to a very different kind of entity—a formal, rational organization staffed by experts who provide a range of specific services. What is especially noteworthy about this transition is that the individual who launched the organization was also responsible for giving it the structure that would permit it to become a lasting organization. Using what social scientists will recognize as a core (Weberian) concept, Dr. Marcus managed to effect the "routinization of (his own) charisma" by laying the foundation for constructing a rational organization. From an organizational theory perspective, Dr. Marcus brought a unique combination of leadership skills to the UAPD.

Question Two: What Can a *Union* Do for Doctors?

The union attracted new members by providing valued services that doctors could not get elsewhere, neither from their professional associations nor very easily from attorneys, consultants, or anyone else. Furthermore, the UAPD developed two parallel sets of services to meet the needs of two different groups of doctors—salaried and private practice physicians.

In representing its salaried members, the union employed traditional union organizing and bargaining tactics. Using this approach, it was able not only to convince salaried doctors of the benefits of membership, but also to convince their employers that the union presence would help rather than hinder the organization. Union representatives intervene early on to prevent problems from becoming bigger and more complex. The level of personal advocacy union staff members are willing to extend makes the UAPD special. Union stewards and business agents affiliated with unions in other sectors fulfill this function. When they "cool out" their own members and keep them from initiating inappropriate grievances, they serve the interests of management as well as the union. Doctors who run into problems in their interactions with the organizations with which they must deal cannot turn to an experienced person who they can count on to intervene on their behalf. UAPD staff provide a unique and valuable service.

The UAPD also serves its private practice members by representing them in negotiations. It does not bargain collectively on their behalf—it is illegal to do so. Instead, it makes comparable services available to members on an individual basis. It does so by developing expertise as it addresses the problems presented by individual members or groups of members. It goes on to share the expertise it acquires with the entire membership. This makes the advice the union offers somewhat similar to the advice its members might obtain on an individual basis from an attorney or business consultant. The difference is that advice from attorneys and consultants comes at a high cost to one person at a time. The cost is even higher if the attorneys and consultants have had little previous experience with the matter at hand.

The expert services the union provides are not easily classified—it functions as a personal advocate, or as a management consulting firm, even a sophisticated self-help organization. Using a health sector analogy, it provides "case management" services for members who are having problems negotiating their way through bureaucractic mazes. Thus, the union represents the interests of doctors on both a collective basis and an individual basis. Because it brings extensive experience to the negotiations between doctors and organizations, it is a position to alter the balance of those negotiations. It has accrued impressive "capital"—a knowledge base—over which it has exclusive control and to which it adds incrementally but continually.

Question Three: Why Do *Doctors* Need a Union?

The answer to this question during the 1970s was somewhat different than it was during the 1980s, and it is changing again during the 1990s in reaction to our ongoing struggle with health care "reform." The short answer is that over the last two decades, doctors' roles and relationships have been transformed from being defined by status to being defined by contract.

Third parties began to play a more prominent role as of the late 1960s, signaling the beginning of the end of the Golden Age of Medicine. Doctors began to complain that third parties were insinuating themselves into the traditional doctor-patient relationship. During the 1980s, the identity of those third parties changed. The third parties increased in size, thereby consolidating the power they were in a position to wield. Although doctors were displeased, they found that they would no longer have patients if they refused to sign contracts—with hospitals, with managed care organizations, with private third-party payers and agencies, and with governmental agencies, namely, Medicare and Medicaid.

So doctors need a union because they need representation in their dealings with large health care organizations. When an individual enters into negotiations with an organization, the organization is obviously in a position to strike the better bargain. Doctors, who had been accustomed to reaching agreements on the basis of trust, largely in negotiations with other individuals, found that they were ill-prepared to enter into negotiations with large organizations. They were even less experienced in adopting to rapidly changing conditions, which has been the state of the health sector for over two decades now (Welsh and Fisher, 1992). With the UAPD behind them, doctors no longer stand alone, inexperienced, and without resources in their negotiations with organizations.

Is the UAPD a Harbinger?

In the introduction I suggested that the UAPD may be a model for other occupational groups. It is certainly a model for doctors in other regions of the country. How many physicians belong to unions or are attempting to establish unions across the country is not clear. By the mid-1980s, there were reports of physicians' unions operating in eight states and in the process of becoming established seven others (Colburn, 1985). However, these unions were not mentioned over the next few years. We can only assume that they faded away. By end of the decade, reports about emergent physicians' unions were again finding their way into the medical press (Trubo, 1989). The UAPD is the only physicians' union that has consistently received attention in the medical press over the last two decades (Meyer and McCormick, 1994; Mangan, 1995).

How the law and the courts will treat this development remains to be seen. Existing legislation clearly states that professionals who are employees have the right to organize and bargain collectively. If they have management responsibilities, they may not. In the meantime, doctors are joining together to form increasingly larger practice groups. It is not at all clear how these groups, and their efforts to establish understandings with health care delivery organizations regarding what are essentially wages and working conditions, will be viewed by the courts. States may decide not to wait for the federal courts to make their views known. They may take the initiative in granting doctors the right to organize and bargain collectively in exchange for cooperation in efforts to contain costs. Efforts to resolve these problems promise to produce considerable turbulence among the participants. They also promise to be very interesting to watch from the sidelines.

Given that medicine has a long-established tradition of serving as the model profession, how it works out its arrangements with the large-scale organizations with which it interacts stands a good chance of having more far-reaching and precedent-setting effects. The UAPD offers an impressive exemplar.

Medicine's move from cottage industry to a modern stage of operations is not an exceptional event. Health sector organizations are becoming increasingly larger, more centralized, and hierarchical; the doctors who interact with them perceive themselves to be more and more divorced from the centers of power where decisions are made without their input and, for that matter, over their objections. But similar observations can be made about work and workers in other sectors.

Some observers are predicting that occupations as such will no longer be influential, that organizations will assume increasing responsibility for organizing work (Bridges, 1994; Abbott, 1989). In my view, such a prediction requires further refinement. It neglects the fact that workers play a role in constructing those arrangements even when they are not (overtly) consulted (Smith, 1994). It is also denies the possibility that workers might choose to recapture the benefits of belonging to an occupational community (Goode, 1957; Heckscher, 1988). Some workers, particularly the more highly skilled who have more bargaining power, may decide to define themselves by craft rather than by firm. The arrangements the medical profession opts to embrace speak to these possibilities.

I have presented the UAPD as an unusual organization, exceptional in its ability to offer a range of new and valued services to its members. In the final chapter, I will look at other white collar and professional unions and occupations, to seek out trends relevant both to doctors and others. The response of these workers to the critical changes in their work lines has attracted relatively little attention. My guess is that this absence of attention is due to the power of entrenched expectations regarding the behavior of American workers. Those who have long relied on the collective loyalty and individual exit options—professionals and white collar employees—are expected to continue doing so, even though their circumstances have changed significantly (Hirschman, 1970). Those who have relied on the collective voice option—that is, on unions—are apparently expected to decline in number and, in the view of some, ultimately in significance. In fact, the collective voice option may be gaining popularity among members of occupational groups who until recently have not felt the need to resort to an organized approach.

❧ 16 ❧

Other Unions and
Their Future

Most discussions of the state of the American labor movement focus on trends affecting blue collar workers. Their loss of power over working conditions is important. But concern about the decline in blue collar union membership is overshadowing the steady rate of increase in other sectors. A larger proportion of the white collar workforce, including professional workers, is now organized than of the blue collar workforce. Particularly among public sector white collar workers, the rate of unionization is increasing. These public employees are engaged in the delivery of services and they work in large, bureaucractic organizations. Having done so for a long time, public sector employees have had more time to develop discontent and mount a response to working in such settings. It is likely that their experiences have some predictive value.

This chapter will present examples that show the range of issues that are galvanizing new union recruits in white collar and other high-skill occupations; explore the various approaches occupational groups are using to gain their objectives; and consider the impact the experience of organizing collectively is having on their respective definitions of their problems. These selected examples do not make for a complete picture of union organizing activities across such occupations; they are a snapshot of a few family members rather than a formal portrait of the entire clan. I will end by hazarding some predictions about the shape of future organizing among doctors and their counterparts in the other professions.

Teachers

The course followed by teachers' unions provides an excellent illustration of the process that shapes professional unions. It shows the evolution of members' expectations regarding worker/management relations and the gradual emergence of a collective voice about issues that go beyond business unionism.

One measure of the success of the teachers' union movement can be found in membership figures. The National Education Association (NEA) claims two million members and the American Federation of Teachers (AFT), an AFL-CIO affiliate, 720,000 (Shostak, 1991). The NEA was established in 1857, but really began to take on the characteristics of a union in the 1960s. The AFT was explicitly organized as a union and chartered by the American Federation of Labor in 1916. According to the president of the National Academy of Education, teachers may have been organized before the 1960s, but they were not united (Angell, 1981).

Teacher activism erupted in the 1960s because of convergence of social forces. With the sudden influx into teaching of young men who were opposed to the Vietnam war, and the social climate of unrest during the 1960s, union activism was seen as an uprising against unresponsive authority inside and outside of schools (Angell, 1981). Increasing bureaucracy and bigness made it harder for teachers to communicate with their employers, school trustees and superintendents, which made them feel less effective (Eberts and Stone, 1985). According to one analysis, the origins of the modern version of teachers' unions can be precisely dated (Kerchner and Mitchell, 1988). The teachers' union movement was born on April 11, 1962, when 20,558 teachers in New York City—that is, more than half—went on strike. The strike lasted one day; an injunction forced the teachers back to work. However, that one-day strike had a lasting effect. It succeeded in establishing collective bargaining as a "professional-labor instrument."

The teachers' union movement changed in response to the emergence of new concerns. The process can be seen as three rather distinct labor relations "generations" (Kerchner and Mitchell, 1988). During the first generation, teachers "met and conferred" with administrators about wages and working conditions. Such meetings were grounded in the premise that all educators shared a common interest in children's education, and, more importantly, that teachers would defer and acquiesce to administrators and school boards.

The second generation is characterized by the recognition of the legitimacy of separate interests on the part of teachers and administrators. Both sides accept the idea that conflict is endemic to the workplace and that conflict management is part of the labor relations process. Teachers engaged in "good faith bargaining" over economic and procedural issues.

The third generation of the teachers' union movement is the "negotiated policy" stage. It acknowledges that teachers have a legitimate interest in negotiating over the functioning of the school on a day-to-day basis. According to Kerchner and Mitchell, it was the shift from the second to the third generation that moved teachers' unions from an industrial to a professional form of unionism.

Airline Pilots

Pilots confronted the issue of professional identity from an unusual perspective. The earliest pilots enjoyed a reputation as daredevils because they were largely employed to perform on exhibition (Hopkins, 1971). As passenger flights became more common, during the 1930s, the pilots recognized that their image would have to change. It was at this point that they began to define themselves as professionals. They did not abandon the mystique that their work was cloaked in glamour. Rather, they cultivated the idea that a pilot holds a person's life in his hands, just like a doctor. Their efforts to develop a professional image were based on the realization that they needed public support to back their efforts to unionize. The professional image helped to achieve that support.

Through the efforts of their union, the Air Line Pilots Association, pilots achieved excellent wages, working conditions, benefits, and the power to influence discussions of air safety. Virtually all pilots employed by the major airlines are now members. More recently, pilots at United Airlines, together with members of some other unions, have succeeded in purchasing a majority share of stock in the airline.

Air Traffic Controllers

Air traffic controllers have not been as fortunate as their colleagues in the cockpit (Shostak and Skocik, 1986). During the early organizing stages, the air traffic controllers took up the issue of whether the organization they were working to establish should be a professional association or a labor union. They decided to ally with the Marine Engineers Beneficial Association (MEBA), a union with a strong record representing a group of professional workers who were also in the transportation industry. The Professional Airline Traffic Controllers Organization (PATCO) gained official recognition in 1972. This marked the first time that the Department of Labor allowed public employees to vote on representation by a labor organization, even though President Kennedy had signed an executive order permitting public employees to organize in 1962.

PATCO's initial concerns revolved around understaffing and compulsory overtime. The same issues were behind the strike of 1981, when President Reagan issued the order to fire 12,000 controllers and broke the union. PATCO could not overcome this blow for a number of reasons. The government supported an accelerated training program for new recruits, used military personnel as strikebreakers, and changed the regulations for landing and entry into key routes. Lack of solidarity from other airline unions and lack of public support also contributed to PATCO's defeat (Edwards, 1986:45).

According to Shostak and Skocik, everyone involved lost as a result of that strike (1986). The workload of air traffic controllers—which is directly related to air safety—has not become any lighter. The result is that the new generation of air traffic controllers, organized in the National Air Traffic Controllers Association, must now address exactly the same issues that PATCO did, namely, working conditions and air safety.

The PATCO strike has had effects that go beyond the industry. One immediate result was that employers from other sectors correctly interpreted the outcome to mean that the Reagan administration would support a more aggressive stance toward strikers. The message for labor has been more complicated. PATCO's defeat clearly illustrates the value of labor solidarity across occupational lines. How unions that attract highly educated white collar and professional workers by focusing on issues specific to their particular occupational groups should react to this lesson is not so clear.

University Professors

Not surprisingly, university professors have not only considered the question of unionization within their own ranks; they have been more interested in publishing their views than the members of some other occupational groups. This literature indicates that there has been a rising interest in unionization and that it is in response to declining morale. Approximately 170,000 professors belong to a union out of the 400,000 full-time and 300,000 part-time faculty (Shostak, 1991).

One study indicates that faculty members' most common reason for joining a union is the perception that they need protection from arbitrary administrative action (Douglas, 1986). Unionized faculty members reported that they joined the union to recover their self-esteem, to overcome demoralization created by administrators who showed little appreciation and recognition of faculty effort. Compensation has been a silent issue at most campuses. Indeed, those affiliated with community colleges seemed very satisfied with their pay.

Although faculty unionization is expected to increase, there is at least one major obstacle, namely, the 1980 *Yeshiva University* ruling by the Supreme Court discussed in Chapter 13. The Court held that faculty members who sit on committees that affect university policy are managerial employees and therefore prohibited from collective bargaining. This decision permitted a number of universities to re fuse to bargain with faculty unions and to institute proceedings leading to decertification. While the NEA, AFL-CIO, and the American Federation of Teachers have continued to lobby Congress for legislation that would permit faculty unions to bargain, in 1988 the Supreme Court confirmed its earlier decision (Shostak, 1991). This ruling has implications for all occupations whose members have a say in management decisions. It is clearly an issue that doctors must consider.

Nurses

Nurses are classified as professionals by the Department of Labor, but they have long fought uphill battles to assert their professionalism at the work site (Levitan and Gallo, 1989). The American Nurses Association (ANA) considered itself a professional association that stood in opposition to collective bargaining until one of its affiliates won a 15 percent increase in 1946. This prompted the ANA to reverse its stance on collective bargaining. Unionization has proceeded slowly. A recent count indicates that approximately one fifth of the 1.6 million registered nurses are covered by labor contracts (Shostak, 1991). They are represented by the ANA, the Service Employees International Union, the American Federation of Teachers, and various local unions.

Both nurses' unions and the ANA struggle to balance the professional interests of nurses, which focus on maintaining high-quality patient care, with occupational interests in income, working conditions, and maintaining control over the scope of their work. Lack of respect for nursing work continues to be a problem. Specific concerns include salary compression, introduction of technology that alters the personal nursing care to which nurses are committed, provision for retraining and developing new skills, and child care assistance. While professional concerns continue to be a high priority, nurses have become increasingly ready to strike. When they do strike, they usually win (Shostak, 1991).

Athletes and Performing Artists

The belief that exceptional talent or skill will go unrecognized and unrewarded makes unions unattractive to many professionals and other white collar workers. The multi-million dollar contracts awarded star athletes and actors who are union members stand as highly visible refutations of that objection. Both professional athletes' unions and performers' unions have succeeded in working out contractual arrangements that consistently improve the salary base and benefits that apply to all members but permit the stars to negotiate individual agreements.

The contractual minimum wage negotiated by the baseball players' union was $109,000 as of 1996. The median salary of baseball players, however, is about half a million dollars, and the average about $1 million. Individual players negotiate these salaries either through arbitration or as free agents. Clearly, the existence of a union contract does not keep [insert the name of your own favorite player] from doing very well for himself.

In football, players also negotiate individually on top of the union contract. There, however, the union made the mistake of agreeing to a salary cap that limits the amount each individual team can pay. This means that players on the same team are competing with each other for a fixed pot of money. It was the baseball owners' attempt to impose such a salary cap on their players that led to the strike of 1994–95.

Similarly, the performing arts unions organized because rank and file performers needed protection. In the early days it was typical for actors to receive no pay for the time they spent rehearsing prior to opening night and to provide their own wardrobes and props. Enforcement of wages and working conditions continues to be the central focus of the performing arts unions: hours, holidays, safety, health insurance, residual payments. But the big names command far more, from personal assistants to a percentage of the gross.

Organizing without Unionizing

As the record of doctors' strikes makes clear, unionization is not a prerequisite for labor action. It helps, of course, to have an organization in place to coordinate activities. But workers—including professionals—can and do take innovative actions that produce improved wages or working conditions, with no union involvement. One example is the steps taken by faculty at an engineering school in New York (Gettleman, 1986).

The story begins when the *Yeshiva University* decision was announced. The administration of the engineering college cut off collective bargaining with the faculty union the same day. The faculty members' longstanding frustration stemmed from what they saw as administrative ineptitude in dealing with fiscal matters. Thus they were particularly galled by the argument on which the *Yeshiva* decision was based—that faculty should not be permitted to engage in collective bargaining because they carry managerial responsibilities. The engineering faculty were continually appalled by the "tidbits" of fiscal data that the administration meted out. In their view, "Mickey Mouse" governance procedures prevented them from doing anything about the organization's financial decision-making. Without the union, they became further demoralized, having no mechanism to capture administrators' attention.

With little to lose, they took steps that were far more innovative than the conservative approach that had characterized their union activities. They agreed that the trustees were the only ones who had the power to make changes and decided to go directly to them. They took advantage of a mechanism that was already in place, a semi-annual lunch to which the members of the Faculty Executive Committee were invited. Such luncheons had traditionally been treated as social events during which faculty did not try to disabuse the trustees of the image of faculty the administration sought to impart—as grumbling, negative, ineffective types. This time, however, they drafted and distributed a report aimed at convincing the trustees that the faculty had serious morale problems and that the administration was responsible. They proposed forming a trustee-administration-faculty committee to consider a morale study.

While the study was the manifest objective, the latent objective was creating the opportunity for faculty to have continuing contact with trustees over the months the committee was scheduled to meet. They were highly successful. The trustees found their insights informative and the solutions they proposed persuasive. The faculty members achieved their objectives.

Some Conclusions and Predictions

Union organizing outside of the industrial sector seems to be taking place behind a media shield. Workers are, of course, aware of organizing activities within their own ranks. However, there is little in the public media about organizing trends across occupations, the issues workers in various occupational areas identify as important, or anything about the innovative mechanisms being implemented to address those issues. That the labor movement, as we have known it, has been fading away, is certainly receiving public attention. The fact that postindustrial unionism exists, however, let alone that it is flourishing, is certain to come as a surprise to many.

The activities of the unions discussed in this chapter, like those of the UAPD, have grown out of the model forged by industrial unionism. However, their activities have moved well beyond that model. While industrial unions succeeded by narrowing the scope of bargaining to wages and working conditions, in order to absorb workers who brought widely varying political and social values to the workplace, postindustrial unions have gained strength by moving in the opposite direction. They have been expanding the range of issues they are willing to take up precisely because their members are eager to have their shared occupational interests addressed.

White collar and professional workers did not join unions in the past because, they said, belonging to a union would deny them the opportunity to be rewarded individually for particularly noteworthy achievements. As is apparent from the UAPD's experience, and that of some of the other unions discussed in this chapter, this fear is not well grounded. Members of white collar and professional unions bring a high level of consensus regarding occupational norms and expectations to their work, which they are ready to translate into union goals; this, in turn, fosters the emergence of innovative mechanisms and forms of representation.

A persistent argument offered by opponents of unionism is that less radical means are available to individuals seeking to achieve work-related objectives than engaging in strikes, which is objectionable because it is unprofessional. But it is the continuity provided by an organizational structure, and not the threat of strikes, that gives workers, especially those who are highly skilled and educated, the means to voice their views on institutional policy—and have that voice acknowledged.

Despite the UAPD's success, I will not predict that doctors will be joining unions in large numbers in the near future. As the drop in AMA membership since its Golden Age clearly indicates, doctors have not exhibited much interest in developing a collective stance. The majority have been slow to take action to challenge their new and dissatisfying conditions of work. So far, the most notable action doctors have taken in any significant number is joining together into increasingly bigger practice groups. This step, however, is more important than it first appears. It is the essential first move required to develop a collective stance. Groups of doctors are moving to the threshold of being able to identify shared interests and act on them.

How soon they decide to take more aggressive steps remains to be seen. Let me be clear. I have no doubt that doctors will take action in response to their growing resentment about being moved closer to employee status and further from the decision-making center—in short, being "managed." I also believe that their actions will receive the attention of a much wider audience. How aggressive or militant those actions are, and whether unions or union-like organizations emerge, is what is difficult to predict. That will vary depending on the number of physicians in an area, the extent of managed care market penetration, the political and social environment, and whether the courts change their interpretation of labor law. How effective doctors are when they do take action will vary as well. However, no one should be surprised if they learn quickly from each other's successes and failures.

A final observation about the unions discussed in this chapter is that they are organized around occupations rather than by firm. This indicates that to identify the "new class" of workers as "intellectual laborers" is missing the mark. Such a label implies that they are more closely attached to the firms that employ them than to their respective occupational identities. Doctors, in my view, come closer to being "intellectual craft workers" who have maintained many of the characteristics of a craft community, even a guild. They do, after all, train new members, develop new skills and techniques within their own ranks, and maintain close ties outside of working hours that reinforce the sense of community.

To the extent that workers in other technically advanced sectors develop a stronger sense of themselves as members of occupational communities, rather than as members of a firm, it is possible that they, too, will proceed to organize along occupational lines rather than by firm. As their discontent rises as they feel increasingly divorced from the decision-making centers of the organizations they work in, organizing collectively around the interests of the occupational community may become considerably more attractive. The highly educated contract workers and consultants, whose connections to the firms that employ them are the most diffuse, may be the first to see the advantages of joining an occupationally based organization that represents their collective interests.

Predicting the implications of the UAPD's experience for unionism in general, and for the physicians' labor movement in particular, requires circumspection. While I cannot say with certainty that the UAPD's success will provide a model for other occupational groups, I am convinced that it has the potential to serve as a harbinger, signaling the emergence of new forms of collective representation. I find it hard to imagine another organization that is in a better position to do so.

Bibliography

Abbott, Andrew. 1989. "The Occupational Structure." *Work and Occupations* 16 (August): 273–291.

Abbott, Andrew. 1988. *The System of Professions: An Essay on the Division of Expert Labor.* Chicago: University of Chicago Press.

Alper, Philip. 1974. "Why I Joined a Union." *Prism* (May): 26–28, 65, 71.

"The AMA Is Not, and Cannot Be, a Union." 1972. *American Medical News* (January 31): reprint, no page.

American Medical Association. 1984. Reference Committee F. *Collective Bargaining Agent for Physicians' Services.* Report L. American Medical Association.

Anderson, Betty Jane. 1972. "Status of Physicians' Unions." Memorandum from the Assistant to the General Counsel to the Executive Vice President, American Medical Association.

Anderson, Odin. 1972. *Health Care: Can There Be Equity? The United States, Sweden, and England.* New York: John Wiley.

Andrews, Mary. 1978. "Housestaff Physicians and Interns Press for Bargaining Rights." *Monthly Labor Review* 101 (August): 30.

Angell, George. 1981. *Faculty and Teacher Bargaining.* Lexington, Mass.: Lexington Books.

Antonovsky, Aaron. 1989. "The Professional-Proletarian Bind: Doctors' Strikes in Western Societies." In *Cross-National Research in Sociology,* edited by Melvin Kohn. Newbury Park, Calif.: Sage.

Appelbaum, Herbert. 1992. *The Concept of Work, Ancient, Medieval, and Modern.* Albany: SUNY Press.

Aronowitz, Stanley. 1979. "The Professional-Managerial Class or Middle Strata." In *Between Labor and Capital,* edited by Pat Wacker. Boston: South End Press.

Attewell, Paul. 1987. "The Deskilling Controversy." *Work and Occupations* 14 (August): 323–346.

Badgley, Robin, and Samuel Wolfe. 1967. *Doctors' Strike.* New York: Atherton.

Baffes, Thomas. 1974. "The Unionization of American Medicine." Unpublished document circulated by the Illinois Physicians Union.

Barnoon, Shlomo, Sara Carmel, and Tsila Zalcman. 1987. "Perceived Health Damages during a Physicians' Strike." *Health Services Research* 22 (June): 141–155.

Bell, Daniel, 1973. *The Coming of Post-Industrial Society.* New York: Basic Books.

Berlant, Jeffrey. 1975. *Profession and Monopoly*. Berkeley: University of California Press.

Bieler, Zoe. 1981. "Quebec: A Lesson in 'Unionized' Medicine." *Canadian Medical Association* (April 15): 1055–1067.

Blackman, Norman. 1973. "Hospital Medical Staff as a Physicians' Union." *New York State Journal of Medicine* (February 1): 466.

Blakeney, Allan. 1993. "The Political Perspective: Planning and Implementing the Canadian System." In *Looking North for Health*, edited by Arnold Bennett and Orvill Adams. San Francisco: Jossey-Bass.

Blaxter, Mildred. 1983. "The Causes of Disease: Women Talking." *Social Science and Medicine* 17: 59–69.

Bledstein, Burton. 1976. *The Culture of Professionalism*. New York: W. W. Norton.

Blendon, Robert, and Drew Altman. 1984. "Public Attitudes About Health-Care Costs." *New England Journal of Medicine* 311 (August 30): 613–616.

Bognanno, Mario, James Dworkin, and Omotayo Fashoyin. 1975. "Physicians' and Dentists' Bargaining Organizations: A Preliminary Look." *Monthly Labor Review* 98 (June): 33–35.

Borzo, Greg. 1994. "Electronic Data Can Make Things Worse Before They Get Better." *American Medical News* (March 28): 1, 6.

Borzo, Greg. 1993. "Ready or Not, EDI Is Coming." *American Medical News* (July 12): 2, 21.

Boston Women's Health Collective. 1971 (revised 1992). *Our Bodies, Our Selves*. New York: Simon and Schuster.

Braverman, Harry. 1974. *Labor and Monopoly Capital*. New York: Monthly Review Press.

Bridges, William. 1994. "The End of the Job." *Fortune* (September): 62–74.

Bruce-Biggs, B. 1979. *The New Class?* New York: McGraw-Hill.

Bucher, Rue, and Joan Stelling. 1977. *Becoming Professional*. Beverly Hills, Calif.: Sage.

Budrys, Grace. 1993. "Coping with Change: Physicians in Prepaid Practice." *Sociology of Health and Illness* 15 (June): 353–374.

Budrys, Grace. 1986. *Planning for the Nation's Health*. New York: Greenwood Press.

Bumke, David. 1987. "Where Doctor Unions Are Finding New Life." *Medical Economics* (December 21): 63–83.

Burnham, John. 1982. "American Medicine's Golden Age: What Happened to It?" *Science* 215 (March 19): 1474–1479.

Burton, Kenneth. 1972. "The Case for a Doctors' Union Now." *Medical Economics* (January 3): 107–112.

Carder, Mack, and Bendix Klingeberg. 1980. "Towards a Salaried Medical Profession: How 'Swedish' was the Seven Crowns Reform?" In *The Shaping of the Swedish Health System*, edited by Arnold Heidensheimer and Nils Elvander. New York: St. Martin's Press.

Chandler, Alfred. 1977. *The Visible Hand: The Managerial Revolution in American Business.* Cambridge, Mass.: Harvard University Press.

Cobble, Dorothy. 1991. *Dishing It Out.* Urbana: University of Illinois Press.

Cohn, Samuel. 1993. *When Strikes Make Sense—and Why.* New York: Plenum Press.

Colburn, Don. 1985. "Physician Organize Thyself." *The Washington Post National Weekly Edition* (August 12): 8.

Cole, Stephen. 1969. *The Unionization of Teachers: A Case Study of the UFT.* New York: Praeger.

"Collective Bargaining by MDs Upheld." 1981. *American Medical News* (April 24): 19.

Cook, Frederick, et al. 1978. "Are White-Collar Trade Unionists Different?" *Sociology of Work and Occupations* 5 (May): 235–245.

Cornfield, Daniel. 1991. "The U.S. Labor Movement: Its Development and Impact on Social Inequality and Politics." *Annual Review of Sociology* 17: 27–49.

Cornfield, Daniel. 1989. "Union Decline and the Political Demands of Organized Labor." *Work and Occupations* 3: 292–322.

Coyne, Patricia. 1980. "Those Militant HMO Doctors." *Private Practice* (April): 59–62.

Cunningham, Robert. 1975. "That's Not What They Had In Mind." *Modern Healthcare* (August): 10, 14, 16.

Daniels, Norman. 1978. "On the Picket Line: Are Doctors' Strikes Ethical?" *Hastings Center Report* 8 (February): 24–29.

Davis, James, and Tom Smith. 1993. *General Social Surveys, 1972–1993: Cumulative Code Book.* Chicago: National Opinion Research Center.

Davis, Karen, and Diane Rowland. 1983. "Uninsured and Underserved: Inequities in Health Care in the United States." *Milbank Memorial Fund Quarterly* 61: 149–176.

de Grandpre, Lili. 1973. "American Medical Unionism. Does Patient or Third Party Retain the Doctor?" *Canadian Medical Association Review* 109 (October 20): 800–805.

DeMaria, Alfred, Dale Tarnowieski, and Richard Gurman. 1972. *Manager Unions?* New York: American Management Association.

Derber, Charles. 1982. *Professionals as Workers: Mental Labor in Advanced Capitalism.* Boston: G. K. Hall.

DeSantis, Grace Budrys. 1980. "Realms of Expertise: A View From Within the Medical Profession." In *Research in the Sociology of Health Care,* Volume 1, edited by Julius Roth. Greenwich, Conn.: JAI Press.

Dohler, Marian. 1989. "Physicians' Professional Autonomy in the Welfare State: Endangered or Preserved?" In *Controlling Medical Professionals, The Comparative Politics of Health Governance,* edited by Giorgio Freddi and James Bjorkman. London: Sage.

Douglas, Joel. 1986. *The Unionized Professorate: A Discriminating Appraisal.* New York: National Center for the Study of Collective Bargaining in Higher Education and the Professions at Baruch College, CUNY.

Eberts, Randall, and Joe Stone. 1986. *Unions and Public Schools.* Lexington, Mass.: Lexington Books.

Edwards, Richard. 1993. *Rights at Work.* New York: Brookings Institution.

Edwards, Richard. 1986. "Unions in Crisis and Beyond: Introduction." In *Unions in Crisis and Beyond, Perspectives from Six Countries,* edited by Richard Edwards, Paolo Garonna, and Franz Todtling. Dover, Mass.: Auburn House.

Edwards, Richard. 1979. *Contested Terrain.* New York: Basic Books.

Edwards, Richard, and Michael Podgursky. 1986. "The Unraveling Accord: American Unions in Crisis." In *Unions in Crisis and Beyond, Perspectives from Six Countries,* edited by Richard Edwards, Paolo Garonna, and Franz Todtling. Dover, Mass.: Auburn House.

Ehrenreich, Barbara, and John Ehrenreich. 1979. "The Professional-Managerial Class." In *Between Labor and Capital,* edited by Pat Wacker. Boston: South End Press.

Ehrenreich, Barbara, and Deirdre English. 1978. *For Her Own Good: 150 Years of the Experts' Advice to Women.* Garden City, N.Y.: Doubleday.

Ehrenreich, Barbara, and Deirdre English. 1973. *Witches, Midwives, and Nurses: A History of Women Healers.* Old Westbury, N.Y.: The Feminist Press.

Eisenberg, John. 1986. *Doctors' Decisions and the Cost of Medical Care.* Ann Arbor, Mich.: Health Administration Press.

Elkind, Pamela Dee. 1991. "Generational Model of Attitudinal Change in Medical Practice." In *Current Research on Occupations and Professions,* edited by Judith Levy. Greenwich, Conn.: JAI Press.

Ellis, Norman. 1982. "The BMA's Trade Union Structure—Four Years On." *British Medical Journal* 285 (July 3).

Ellwood, Paul, et al. 1971. "Health Maintenance Strategy." *Medical Care* 9 (May–June): 291–299.

Engel, Gloria. 1970. "Professional Autonomy and Bureaucratic Organization." *Administrative Science Quarterly* 15 (March): 12–21.

Engel, Gloria, and Richard Hall. 1973. "The Growing Industrialization of the Professions." In *The Professions and Their Prospects,* edited by Eliot Freidson. Beverly Hills, Calif.: Sage.

Engel, Gloria, et al. 1979. "Professionals and Unionization: A Study of Two Cohorts of Physician Housestaff." *Evaluation and the Health Professions* 2 (September): 331–355.

Epstein, Arnold. 1993. "Changes in the Delivery of Care Under Comprehensive Health Care Reform." *New England Journal of Medicine* 329 (November 25): 1672–1676.

Erickson, Kai. 1990. "On Work and Alienation." In *The Nature of Work*, edited by Kai Erickson and Steven Peter Vallas. New Haven: Yale University Press.

Estill, Jerry. 1993. "From Inside the System: A Physician, Hospital Administrator, and Business Executive Talk about Their Work in Canada." In *Looking North for Health*, edited by Arnold Bennett and Orvill Adams. San Francisco: Jossey-Bass.

Evans, Robert. 1986. "Finding the Levers, Finding the Courage: Lessons from Cost Containment in North America." *Journal of Health Politics, Policy and Law* 11: 585–615.

Fehr, Donald. 1986. "Labor Relations in Baseball." In *The Unionized Professorate: A Discriminating Appraisal*, edited by Joel Douglas. New York: National Center for the Study of Collective Bargaining in Higher Education and the Professions at Baruch College, CUNY.

Feldstein, Martin. 1981. *Hospital Costs and Hospital Insurance*. Cambridge, Mass., Harvard University Press.

Ferber, Stanly. 1973. "Doctors' Unions—Down and Out?" *Medical Economics* (September 17): 45–58.

Ferber, Stanly. 1972. "Medicine's Union Leaders Lay It on the Line." *Medical Economics* (July 17): 57–61.

Fligstein, Neil. 1990. *The Transformation of Corporate Control*. Cambridge, Mass.: Harvard University Press.

Form, William. 1987. "On the Degradation of Skills." *Annual Review of Sociology* 13: 29–47.

Freeman, Richard. 1985. "Why Are Unions Faring Poorly in NLRB Representation Elections?" In *Challenges and Choices Facing American Labor*, edited by Thomas Kochan. Cambridge, Mass.: MIT Press.

Freeman, Richard, and James Medoff. 1984. *What Do Unions Do?* New York: Basic Books.

Freidson, Eliot. 1994. *Professionalism Reborn*. Chicago: University of Chicago Press.

Freidson, Eliot. 1986. *Professional Powers*. Chicago: University of Chicago Press.

Freidson, Eliot. 1973. "Professionalization and the Organization of Middle-Class Labour in Post-Industrial Society." In *Professionalization and Social Change*, edited by Paul Halmos. Keele, Staffordshire: University of Keele.

Freidson, Eliot. 1970a. *Professional Dominance*. Chicago: Aldine de Gruyter.

Freidson, Eliot. 1970b. *Profession of Medicine*. New York: Dodd, Mead.

"FTC Drops Antitrust Probe of California Physicians' Union." 1990. *Modern Healthcare* (October 22): 58.

Galbraith, John Kenneth. 1967. *The New Industrial State*. Boston: Houghton Mifflin.

Gamble, Stephen. 1976. "Coping with a Strike by Doctors." *Hospitals* (September 1): 61–64.

Garbarino, Joseph. "Emergence of Collective Bargaining." 1973. In *Faculty Unions and Collective Bargaining*, edited by E.D. Duryea and Robert Fisk. San Francisco: Jossey-Bass.

Garceau, Oliver. 1941. *The Political Life of the American Medical Association*. Cambridge, Mass.: Harvard University Press.

Garfinkel, Simson. 1989. "An Interview with Sanford Marcus, MD." *Internal Medicine World Report* 4 (September 15–30): 1.

Garson, Barbara. 1988. *The Electronic Sweatshop*. New York: Simon and Schuster.

Geisen, Gerald. 1983. *Professions and Professional Ideologies in America*. Chapel Hill: University of North Carolina Press.

Gettleman, Marvin. 1986. "Polytechnic Institute of New York." In *The Unionized Professorate: A Discriminating Appraisal*, edited by Joel Douglas. New York: National Center for the Study of Collective Bargaining in Higher Education and the Professions at Baruch College, CUNY.

Ginzberg, Eli. 1990. *The Medical Triangle: Physicians, Politicians and the Public*. Cambridge, Mass.: Harvard University Press.

Ginzberg, Eli. 1985. *American Medicine: The Power Shift*. New York: Rowan and Allanheld.

Ginzberg, Eli. 1982. "Procompetition in Health Care." Milbank Memorial Fund Quarterly 60 (Summer): 386–398.

Godt, Paul. 1987. "Confrontation, Consent, and Corporatism: State Strategies and the Medical Profession in France, Great Britain, and West Germany." *Journal of Health, Politics, Policy and Law* 12 (Fall): 459–480.

Goode, William. 1957. "Community within a Community." *American Sociological Review* 22: 194–200.

Gordon, David, Richard Edwards, and Michael Reich. 1982. *Segmented Work, Divided Workers*. Cambridge: Cambridge University Press.

Gotbaum, Victor. 1993. "Foreword." In *Union Voices*, edited by Glenn Adler and Doris Suarez. New York: SUNY Press.

Gouldner, Alvin. 1979. *The Future of Intellectuals and the Rise of the New Class*. New York: Seabury Press.

Gray, Bradford. 1991. *The Profit Motive and Patient Care*. Cambridge, Mass.: Harvard University Press.

Greco, Peter, and John Eisenberg. 1993. "Changing Physicians' Practices." *New England Journal of Medicine* 329 (October 21): 1271–1274.

Greenberg, Warren. 1978. *Competition in the Health Care Sector: Past, Present, and Future*. Proceedings of a Conference Sponsored by the Bureau of Economics, Federal Trade Commission. Washington, D.C.: U.S. Government Printing Office.

"Group Health Doctors Elect Union as Bargaining Agent." 1978. In *Health Manpower Report*. Washington, D.C.: Capital Publications.

Haber, Samuel. 1991. *The Quest for Authority and Honor in the American Professions 1750–1900*. Chicago: University of Chicago Press.

Hafferty, Frederic. 1988. "Theories at the Crossroads: A Discussion of Evolving Views on Medicine as a Profession." *The Milbank Quarterly* 66, Supplement 2: 202–225.

Hafferty, Frederic, and John McKinlay. 1993. *The Changing Medical Profession*. New York: Oxford University Press.

Halberstam, Michael. 1973. "Unionism: The Newest Trap for American Doctors." *Medical Economics* (April 16): 75–78.

Hall, Oswald. 1946. "The Informal Organization of the Medical Profession." *Canadian Journal of Economics and Political Science* 12 (February): 30–41.

Hall, Richard. 1987. *Organizations: Structures, Processes, and Outcomes*. Englewood Cliffs, N.J.: Prentice-Hall.

Hall, Richard. 1975. *Occupations and the Social Structure*, Englewood Cliffs, N.J.: Prentice-Hall.

Halmos, Paul. 1973. *Professionalisation and Social Change*. Keele, Staffordshire: University of Keele.

Hargrove, Barbara. 1986. *The Emerging New Class*. New York: Pilgrim Press.

Harrington, Michael. 1972. "Old Working Class, New Working Class." *Dissent* 19: 146–162.

Harrison, Michael. 1991. "A Profession in Conflict: Union Militancy Among Israeli Physicians." In *Current Research on Occupations and Professions*, edited by Judith Levy. Greenwich, Ct.: JAI Press.

Harrison, Stephen. 1988. *Managing the National Health Service*. London: Chapman and Hall.

Hattam, Victoria. 1993. *Labor Visions and State Power: The Origins of Business Unionism in the United States*. Princeton: Princeton University Press.

Haug, Marie. 1994. "Elderly Patients, Caregivers, and Physicians: Theory and Research on Health Care Triads." *Journal of Health and Social Behavior* 35 (March): 1–12.

Haug, Marie. 1988. "A Re-examination of the Hypothesis of Physician Deprofessionalization." *The Milbank Quarterly* 66, Supplement 2: 48–56.

Haug, Marie. 1973. "Deprofessionalization: An Alternative Hypothesis for the Future." In *Professionalisation and Social Change*, edited by Paul Halmos. Keele, Staffordshire: University of Keele.

Health Manpower Report. 1978. Washington, D.C.: Capital Publications.

Heckscher, Charles. 1988. *The New Unionism*. New York: Basic Books.

Heidenheimer, Arnold, and Lars Johansen. 1985. "Organized Medicine and Scandinavian Professional Unionism: Hospital Policies and Exit Options in Denmark and Sweden." *Journal of Health Politics, Policy, and Law* 10 (Summer): 347–370.

Hirsch, Barry, and David McPherson. 1993. "Union Membership and Coverage Files from the Current Population Surveys: Note." *Industrial and Labor Relations Review* 46 (April): 574–578.

Hirschman, Albert. 1970. *Exit, Voice, and Loyalty.* Cambridge, Mass.: Harvard University Press.

Hoffman, Eileen. 1976. *Unionization of Professional Societies.* New York: The Conference Board.

Holoweiko, Mark. 1983. "One Doctors' Union Hangs On." *Medical Economics* (October 3): 206, 210.

Hopkins, George. 1971. *The Airline Pilots: A Study in Elite Unionization.* Cambridge, Mass.: Harvard University Press.

Horty, John. 1975. "When Is a Doctor an Employee?" *Modern Healthcare* (September): 72–74.

"Housestaff Group's Union Rights Upheld by U.S. Labor Panel." 1982. *American Medical News* (May 7):10.

Hsiao, William, et al. 1988. "Resource-Based Relative Values." *Journal of the American Medical Association* 260 (October 28): 2347–2360.

Hueppe, Frederick. 1973. "Private University: St. Johns." In *Faculty Unions and Collective Bargaining,* edited by E.D. Duryea and Robert Fisk. San Francisco: Jossey-Bass.

Hughes, Everett. 1958. *Men and Their Work.* Glencoe, Ill.: Free Press.

Iglehart, John. 1991. "Health Policy Report: Germany's Health Care System." *New England Journal of Medicine* 324 (February 14): 503–508.

Illich, Ivan. 1976. *Medical Nemesis.* London: Calder and Boyars.

Ito, Hirobumi. 1980. "Health Insurance and Medical Services in Sweden and Denmark 1850–1950." In *The Shaping of the Swedish Health System,* edited by Arnold Heidenheimer and Nils Elvander. New York: St. Martin's Press.

Jackson, Pamela, and Roger Clark. 1987. "Collective Bargaining and Faculty Compensation: Faculty as a New Working Class." *Sociology of Education* 60 (October): 242–256.

Jacoby, Sanford. 1985. *Employing Bureaucracy.* New York: Columbia University Press.

Jellinek, Michael, and Barry Nurcombe. 1993. "Two Wrongs Don't Make a Right." *Journal of the American Medical Association* 270 (October 13): 1737–1739.

Jensen, Joyce. 1987. "If Forced to Change Positions, Most Physicians Say They Would Remain in the Healthcare Field." *Modern Healthcare* (November 20): 64–65.

Johnson, Dirk. 1987. "Doctors' Dilemma, Unionizing." *New York Times* (July 13): D1, D4.

Johnson, Kirk. 1989. "MD Unions Not Cure-All in Negotiation." *American Medical News* (February 3):24–25.

Johnsson, Julie. 1993. "Conquering the Contract Dragon." *American Medical News* (March 8):13–14.

Kantor, Rosabeth Moss. 1990. "The New Work Force Meets the Changing Work Place." In *The Nature of Work,* edited by Kai Erickson and Steven Peter Vallas. New Haven: Yale University Press.

Kantor, Rosabeth Moss. 1989. *When Giants Learn to Dance.* New York: Simon and Schuster.

Kerchner, Charles, and Douglas Mitchell. 1988. *The Changing Idea of a Teachers' Union.* London: The Falmer Press.

Kessler-Harris, Alice. 1987. "Trade Unions Mirror Society in Conflict between Collectivism and Individualism." *Monthly Labor Review* 110 (August): 32–35.

Kimball, Bruce. 1992. *The "True Professional Ideal" in America.* Cambridge: Blackwell.

Kirn, Timothy. 1992. "Will You Take An IOU?" *American Medical News* (August 3): 1, 40.

Klover, Jon, David Stephens, and Vincent Luchsinger. 1980. "Contemporary Perceptions of Unionization in the Medical Profession: A Study of Attitudes of Unionized and Non-Union Physicians." *Journal of Collective Negotiations* 9: 107–117.

Kochan, Thomas. 1985. *Challenges and Choices Facing American Labor.* Cambridge, Mass.: MIT Press.

Kochan, Thomas. 1979. "How American Workers View Labor Unions." *Monthly Labor Review* (April): 23–31.

Kraft, Philip. 1977. *Programmers and Managers: The Routinization of Computer Programming in the United States.* New York: Springer-Verlag.

Krause, Elliot. 1988. "Doctors, Partitocrazia, and the Italian State." *The Milbank Quarterly* 66, Supplement 2: 148–166.

Larkin, Howard. 1995. "You're Fired." *American Medical News* (February 13): 11–12.

Larkin, Howard. 1993. "Welcome to the Machine." *American Medical News* (January 4): 27–28.

Larson, Magli Sarfatti. 1980. "Proletarianization and Educated Labor." *Theory and Society* 9 (January): 131–175.

Larson, Magli Sarfatti. 1977. *The Rise of Professionalism.* Berkeley: University of California Press.

Lefton, Doug. 1981a. "Canadian MDs Eyeing Collective Bargaining." *American Medical News* (September 4): 3, 22.

Lefton, Doug. 1981b. "Quebec MDs Battling New Federal Curbs." *American Medical News* (December 11): 3, 8.

Leicht, Kevin, Mary Fennell, and Kristine Witkowski. 1995. "The Effects of

Hospital Characteristics and Radical Organizational Change on the Relative Standing of Healthcare Professionals." *Journal of Health and Social Behavior* 36 (June): 151–167.

Levitan, Sar, and Frank Gallo. 1989. "Collective Bargaining and Private Sector Professionals." *Monthly Labor Review* (September): 24–33.

Levy, Judith. 1991. *Current Research on Occupations and Professions.* Greenwich, Ct.: JAI Press.

Leyerle, Betty. 1994. *The Private Regulation of American Health Care.* Armonk, N.Y.: M.E. Sharpe.

Leyerle, Betty. 1984. *Moving and Shaking American Medicine.* Westport, Ct.: Greenwood Press.

Liebfried, Stephen, and Florian Tennstedt. 1986. "Health Insurance Policy and Berufsverbote in the Nazi Takeover." In *Political Values on Health Care: The German Experience,* edited by Donald Light and Alexander Schuller. Cambridge: MIT Press.

Liebowitz, Barry. 1986. "The Physicians." In *The Unionized Professorate: A Discriminating Appraisal,* edited by Joel Douglas. New York: National Center for the Study of Collective Bargaining in Higher Education and the Professions at Baruch College, CUNY.

Light, Donald. 1986. "Corporate Medicine for Profit." *Scientific American* 255 (6): 38–45.

Light, Donald, and Sol Levine. 1988. "The Changing Nature of the Medical Profession: A Theoretical Overview." *The Milbank Quarterly* 66, Supplement 2: 10–32.

Light, Donald, and Alexander Schuller, eds. 1986. *Political Values on Health Care: The German Experience.* Cambridge: MIT Press.

Linder, Marc. 1992. *Farewell to the Self-Employed.* New York: Greenwood.

Lipset, Seymour Martin. 1986. "North American Labor Movements: A Comparative Perspective." In *Unions in Transition,* edited by Seymour Martin Lipset. San Francisco: Institute for Contemporary Studies Press.

Lomas, J., and A. P. Constandriopoulos. 1994. "Regulating Limits to Medicine: Towards Harmony in Public- and Self-Regulation." In *Why Are Some People Healthy and Others Not?,* edited by Robert Evans, Morris Barer, and Theodore Marmor. New York: Aldine de Gruyter.

Luft, Harold. 1987. *Health Maintenance Organizations.* New Brunswick, N.J.: Transaction Books.

Lumley, Roger. 1973. *White-Collar Unionism in Britain.* London: Methuen and Co.

Mallet, Serge. 1975. *Essays on the New Working Class.* Edited and translated by Dick Howard and Dean Savage. St. Louis: Telos Press.

Mangan, Doreen. 1995. "Will Doctor Unions Finally Take Hold?" *Medical Economics* (July 24):115–120.

Marcus, Sanford, 1989a. "Let's Shuck Medicine's Ridiculous Armor." *Medical Tribune* (February): 1.

Marcus, Sanford. 1989b. "Wages Would Restore Physicians' Dignity." *Health Week* (May 1): reprint, no page.

Marcus, Sanford. 1986a. "A Proposal for the Defense of the American Medical Profession." *Journal of Miami Medicine* (February): 21–22.

Marcus, Sanford. 1986b. "A Proposal for Unions as a Device for the Defense of the American Medical Profession." *North Carolina Medical Journal* 27 (September) 403–407.

Marcus, Sanford. 1985. "How about a Truce in the War on Doctors?" *Los Angeles Health Care*/Western-Central Edition (Summer): reprint, no page.

Marcus, Sanford. 1984a. "Trade Unionism for Doctors: An Idea Whose Time Has Come." *New England Journal of Medicine* 311 (December 6): 1508–1511.

Marcus, Sanford. 1984b. "Saving an Honored Profession from Extinction?" *Private Practice* (December): 41–44.

Marcus, Sanford. 1975a. "The Time Has Come to Bargain for Higher Incomes." *Medical Economics* (March 17): 204–214.

Marcus, Sanford. 1975b. "The Purposes of Unionization in the Medical Profession: The Unionized Profession's Perspective in the United States." *International Journal of Health Services* 5: 37–42.

Marcus, Sanford. 1973. "Physicians' Unions—Pro and Con." *American Medical News* (April 30): 5.

Maressa, Vincent. 1986. "Practical and Legal Considerations: Collective Bargaining." *New Jersey Medicine* 83 (February): 82.

Marmor, Theodore, Mark Schlesinger, and Richard Smithey. 1987. "Nonprofit Organizations and Health Care." In *The Nonprofit Sector*, edited by Walter Powell. New Haven: Yale University Press.

Martinelli, Alberto, and Neil Smelser. 1990. "Economic Sociology: Historical Threads and Analytical Issues." In *Economy and Society: Overview of Economic Sociology*, edited by Alberto Martinelli and Neil Smelser. London: Sage.

McCormick, Brian. 1993a. "British Columbia MDs Eye Union." *American Medical News* (May 17): 3, 30.

McCormick, Brian. 1993b. "Pressured by Managed Care?" *American Medical News* (May 3): 1, 31.

McCormick, Brian. 1993c. "AMA Writes to Congress about Collective Negotiation." *American Medical News* (September 21): 4.

McCormick, Brian. 1992. "Doctors' Place at the Bargaining Table." *American Medical News* (September 14): 3, 44, 47.

McCraken, Richard. 1986. Document authored by the legal firm Davis, Cowell and Bowe, on behalf of the UAPD.

McKinlay, John. 1977. "The Business of Good Doctoring or Doctoring as Good

Business: Reflections in Freidson's View of the Medical Game." *International Journal of Health Services* 7:459–483.

McKinlay, John. 1973. "On the Professional Regulation of Change." In *Professionalisation and Social Change*, edited by Paul Halmos. Keele, Staffordshire: University of Keele.

McKinlay, John, and Joan Arches. 1985. "Towards the Proletarianization of Physicians." *International Journal of Health Services* 15: 161–195.

Meiskins, Peter, and Chris Smith. 1993. "Organizing Engineering Work." *Sociology of Work and Occupations* 20 (May): 123–146.

Meyer, Harris. 1993a. "Fee for Service Dying as Big Doctor Groups Take Over L.A." *American Medical News* (April 12): 1, 5, 6.

Meyer, Harris. 1993b. "Vermont Leaning toward Single-Payer; Budget Target Set." *American Medical News* (July 26): 3, 29.

Meyer, Harris, 1993c. "New Health Care Cost Controls Are Approved in Germany." *American Medical News* (February 15): 9.

Meyer, Harris. 1992. "Doctor Strike over Strict Cap Heralds New Era in Canada." *American Medical News* (August 3): 3, 13.

Meyer, Harris. 1989a. "Collective Bargaining by MDs 'One of Hottest' Antitrust Issues—FTC." *American Medical News* (December 22–29): 1, 40, 41.

Meyer, Harris. 1989b. "Official: Private Physician Unions May Undergo Antitrust Probe." *American Medical News* (March 24–31): 1, 37.

Meyer, Harris. 1987. "Twin Cities' MDs Put Out Union Feelers in Fee Feud." *American Medical News* (April 3): 3.

Meyer, Harris, and Brian McCormick. 1994. "Florida Doctors' Union Tests Bargaining Limits." *American Medical News* (December 5): 1, 35.

Meyer, John. 1986. "Institutional and Organizational Rationalization in the Mental Health System." In *The Organization of Mental Illness Services*, edited by W. Richard Scott and Bruce Black. Beverly Hills, Calif.: Sage.

Mitka, Mike. 1995. "HMO 'Stampede' Celebrates Big Enrollment Gains." *American Medical News* (July 24): 5.

Mitka, Mike. 1993. "Merging for Managed Care." *American Medical News* (July 19): 2.

Mitka, Mike. 1992. "Will HMOs Create Physician Glut?" *American Medical News* (May 18): 15, 18.

Moore, Dick. 1986. "Actors' Unions." In *The Unionized Professorate: A Discriminating Appraisal*, edited by Joel Douglas. New York: National Center for the Study of Collective Bargaining in Higher Education and the Professions at Baruch College, CUNY.

Navarro, Vicente. 1988. "Professional Dominance or Proletarianization? Neither." *The Milbank Quarterly* 66, Supplement 2: 57–75.

Navarro, Vicente. 1986. "Medical History as Justification Rather than Explanation: A Critique of Paul Starr's 'The Social Transformation of Medicine'." In *Crisis, Health, and Medicine*. edited by Vicente Navarro. New York: Tavistock.

Oberman, Linda. 1994. "Changing Neighborhood." *American Medical News* (November 28): 3, 6, 7.

Oberman, Linda. 1993. "AMA Has Record Membership; Looks to Market Share Gains." *American Medical News* (February 22): 35.

Owens, Arthur. 1987. "What Competition Is Doing to Earnings." *Medical Economics* (January 5): 158–177.

Page, Leigh. 1990. "California Residents Union Joins AFL-CIO Affiliate." *American Medical News* (October 19): 1, 33.

Pantell, Robert, and Charles Irwin. 1979. "Appendectomies During Physicians' Boycott." *Journal of the American Medical Association* 242 (October 12): 1627–1630.

Parsons, Talcott. 1951. *The Social System*. New York: Free Press.

Perrow, Charles. 1986. *Complex Organizations: A Critical Essay*. New York: Random House.

Pfeffer, Jeffrey, and Alison Davis-Blake. 1990. "Unions and Job Satisfaction: An Alternative View." *Work and Occupations* 17 (August): 259–283.

"Physicians Join Union." 1993. *American Medical News* (October 25): 30.

Pinkney, Deborah. 1992. "California Law Gives Nurses New Prescribing Authority." *American Medical News* (January 20): 1, 29.

Piore, Michael. 1985. "Computer Technologies, Market Structure, and Strategic Union Choices." In *Challenges and Choices Facing American Labor*, edited by Thomas Kochan. Cambridge: MIT Press.

Piore, Michael, and Charles Sabel. 1984. *The Second Industrial Divide*. New York: Basic Books.

"Radiologists Lose Privileges in Dispute." 1980. *American Medical News* (September 26): 7.

Rankin, Tom. 1990. *New Forms of Work Organization: The Challenge for North American Unions*. Toronto: University of Toronto Press.

Rayack, Elton. 1967. *Professional Power and American Medicine: The Economics of the American Medical Association*. Cleveland: World.

Reich, Robert. 1991. *The Work of Nations: Preparing Ourselves for the 21st Century*. New York: Alfred Knopf.

Relman, Arnold. 1993. "Medical Practice under the Clinton Reforms—Avoiding Domination by Business." *New England Journal of Medicine* 329 (November 18): 1574–1576.

Relman, Arnold. 1980. "The New Medical-Industrial Complex." *New England Journal of Medicine* 303 (October 23): 963–970.

Relman, Arnold. 1979. "Is It Better with a Union Doctor?" *New England Journal of Medicine* 301 (July 19): 156–158.

Richardson, William. 1941. "Union Cards for Doctors?" *Medical Economics* (March): 56–58, 88.

Richmond, Julius, and Rashi Fein. 1995. "The Health Care Mess." *Journal of the American Medical Association* 273 (January 6): 69–71.

Riska, Elianne. 1988. "The Professional Status of Physicians in the Nordic Countries." *The Milbank Quarterly* 66, Supplement 2: 133–147.

Ritzer, George. 1993. *The McDonaldization of Society.* Thousand Oaks, Calif.: Pine Forge Press.

Ritzer, George, and David Walczak. 1988. "Rationalization and the Deprofessionalization of Physicians." *Social Forces* 67 (September): 1–22.

Ritzer, George, and David Walczak. 1986. *Working: Conflict and Change.* Englewood Cliffs, N.J.: Prentice-Hall.

Robinson, James. 1991. "HMO Penetration and Hospital Cost Inflation in California." *Journal of the American Medical Association* 266 (November 20): 2719–2723.

Roemer, Milton. 1991. *National Health Systems of the World.* Volume I. New York: Oxford University Press.

Roemer, Milton. 1986. "Proletarianization of or Organization of Health Services?" *International Journal of Health Services* 16:469–471.

Rosman, Joseph. 1975. "One Year under Taft-Hartley." *Hospitals* (December 16): 64–68.

Rubin, Beth. 1986. "Class Struggle American Style: Unions, Strikes, and Wages." *American Sociological Review* 51 (October): 618–631.

Rueschemeyer, Dietrich. 1983. "Professional Autonomy and the Social Control of Expertise." In *The Sociology of the Professions,* edited by Robert Dinewall and Philip Strong. London: Macmillan.

Ruzek, Sheryl. 1979. *The Women's Health Movement.* New York: Preager.

Saltman, Richard. 1990. "Competition and Reform in the Swedish Health System." *The Milbank Quarterly* 68: 597–618.

Sammons, James. 1976. "American Medical Association Explains Negotiation Department." *Hospitals* (May 16): 113–115.

Scheier, Ronni. 1986. "Twin Cities HMO Sues MD Critics." *American Medical News* (June 20): reprint, no page.

Schwartz, William. 1970. "Medicine and the Computer." *New England Journal of Medicine* 283 (December): 1255–1264.

Shortell, Stephen. 1973. "Patterns of Referral Among Internists in Private Practice." *Journal of Health and Social Behavior* 14 (December): 335–348.

Shortell, Stephen, Rovin Gillies, and Kelly Devers. 1995. "Reinventing the American Hospital." *The Milbank Quarterly* 73: 131–160.

Shostak, Arthur. 1991. *Robust Unionism.* Ithaca, N.Y.: ILR Press.

Shostak, Arthur, and David Skocik. 1986. *The Air Controllers' Controversy, Lessons from the PATCO Strike.* New York: Human Services Press.

Shryrock, Richard. 1947. *The Development of Modern Medicine: An Interpretation of the Social and Scientific Factors*. New York: Alfred Knopf.

Sloan, Frank, and Joseph Valvona. 1986. "Why Has Hospital Length of Stay Declined? An Evaluation of Alternative Theories." *Social Science and Medicine* 22: 63–73.

Smith, Tom. 1981. *Can We Have Confidence in Confidence? Revisited*. Washington, D.C.: Bureau of the Census.

Smith, Vicki. 1994. "Braverman's Legacy." *Work and Occupations* 21 (November): 403–421.

Sobal, Larry, and James Hepner. 1990. "Physician Unions: Any Doctor Can Join, but Who Can Bargain Collectively?" *Hospital and Health Services Administration* 35 (Fall): 327–340.

Somerville, Janice. 1994. "Single Payer Referendum Set." *American Medical News* (May 16): 3, 10, 11.

Spek, Jan-Erik. 1990. "Why Is the System So Costly? Problems of Policy and Management at the National and Regional Levels." In *The Shaping of the Swedish Health System*, edited by Arnold Heidenheimer and Nils Elvander. New York: St. Martin's Press.

Starr, Paul. 1982. *The Social Transformation of American Medicine*. New York: Basic Books.

"Stats." 1992. *American Medical News* (June 15): 18.

Steele, Mark. 1976. "AMA Teaches Physicians to Fight Back." *Modern Healthcare* (July): 31–34.

Stevens, Rosemary. 1989. *In Sickness and in Wealth*. New York: Basic Books.

Stevens, Rosemary. 1971. *American Medicine and the Public Interest*. New Haven: Yale University Press.

Stoeckle, John. 1988. "Reflections on Modern Doctoring." *The Milbank Quarterly* 66, Supplement 2: 76–91.

Stone, Deborah. 1980. *The Limits of Professional Power*. Chicago: University of Chicago Press.

Strand, David, and Ruth Mickelsen. 1990. "Should Doctors of the World Unite?" *Managed HealthCare* (April 9): 23.

Tomkins, Christopher. 1982. *The State of the Unions*. Cambridge: Cambridge University Press.

Touraine, Alain. 1971. *The Postindustrial Society*. New York: Random House.

Trubo, Richard. 1989. "Doctors' Unions." *Medical World News* (July 10): 28–34.

Turner, Lowell. 1991. *Democracy at Work: Changing World Markets and the Future of Labor Unions*. Ithaca, N.Y.: Cornell University Press.

Ulrich, Sylvia. 1973. "Will Your Appendectomy Be Performed by a Member of the AFL-CIO?" *Modern Hospital* 121 (October): 63–67.

"Union Contract Binds Hospital to MD Review Only." 1973. *American Medical News* (March 5): reprint, no page.

"Unions Opposed." 1973. *American Medical News* (April 30): 1, 7.

U.S. Department of Labor. 1995. *Employment and Earnings* 41 (January): 216.

U.S. General Accounting Office. 1995. *Medicaid Section 1115 Waivers.* Report to the Ranking Minority Member, Committee on Finance, U.S. Senate. Washington, D.C.

Weber, Max. 1946. *From Max Weber: Essays in Sociology.* Edited and translated by H.H. Gerth and C. Wright Mills. New York: Oxford University Press.

Weisman, Ellen. 1987. "Swedish Physicians Win Salary Increase." *American Medical News* (January 16): 33.

Welsh, H. Gilbert, and Elliott Fisher. 1992. "Negotiating a Settlement between Physicians and Society." *New England Journal of Medicine* 327 (October 29): 1312–1315.

White, Harrison. 1992. *Identity and Control: A Structural Theory of Social Action.* Princeton: Princeton University Press.

Willis, Evan. 1988. "Doctoring in Australia: A View at the Bicentenary." *The Milbank Quarterly* 66, Supplement 2: 167–181.

Wolfe, Samuel. 1975. "Worker Conflicts in the Health Field: An Overview." *International Journal of Health Services* 5: 5–8.

Wolinsky, Frederic. 1993. "The Professional Dominance, Deprofessionalization, Proletarianization, and Corporatization Perspective: An Overview and Synthesis." In *The Changing Medical Profession,* edited by Frederic Hafferty and John McKinlay. New York: Oxford University Press.

Wolinsky, Frederic. 1988. "The Professional Dominance Perspective, Revisited." *The Milbank Quarterly* 66, Supplement 2: 33–47.

Wolinsky, Howard. 1980. "Canadian MDs Hit Federal Report, Eye Possibility of Forming Union." *American Medical News* (September 26): 4.

Index

Abbott, Andrew, 38, 143
airline pilots, 53–55, 147
air traffic controllers, 147–148
AFL-CIO, 12, 48–49, 102–103, 146, 149
Alper, Philip, 15
Altman, Drew, 33n, 61
American Federation of Physicians and
    Dentists, 16, 49–50
American Federation of State, County and
    Municipal Employees (AFSCME), 52
American Medical Association (AMA):
    alternatives to unionism, 56–58, 86–93
    assistance to members, 13–14, 92–93,
        136
    and collective bargaining, 117–119,
        124–125
    and health reform, 29
    membership figures, 87, 153
    stance on unionism, 17, 19, 90, 117–118
American Physicians Guild, 14
American Physicians Union of Texas, 13
Anderson, Odin, 26
Andrews, Mary, 123
Angell, George, 146
Antonovsky, Aaron, 21, 27, 30
Arches, Joan, 34n, 71, 98–99
athletes and performing artists, 150–151
Attewell, Paul, 101
autonomy of physicians, 13, 36, 72, 98

Badgley, Robin, 22
Baffes, Thomas, 117
bargaining rights of residents and interns,
    123–124
Bell, Daniel, 109, 112
Berlant, Jeffrey, 33, 34n
Blackman, Norman, 122
Blakeney, Allen, 22

Blaxter, Mildred, 44
Bledstein, Burton, 34, 37
Blendon, Robert, 33n, 64
Bognanno, Mario, 11, 95
Borzo, Greg, 68
Boston Women's Health Collective, 11
Braverman, Harry, 100
Bridges, William, 143
Bruce-Biggs, B., 109
Bucher, Rue, 98n
Budrys, Grace, 37, 43n, 60n, 64n, 87n
Bumke, David, 11, 126
bureaucratization, 34n, 72, 98–99,
    107–111
Burnham, John, 38–39
Burton, Kenneth, 13–16, 88

California Medical Association, 19–20,
    93–95, 139
capitalism, 34n, 99, 104
Carder, Mack, 26
Clark, Roger, 96n
Clayton Act, 114
Cobble, Dorothy, 103
Colburn, Don, 2, 142
collective bargaining, 95
    legality of, 114
collective bargaining by doctors, 140
    and AMA, 90, 93, 124. See also American
        Medical Association
    in California, 51–52, 130
    in Canada, 29
    in Israel, 27–28
    in Scandinavian countries, 26
    in United Kingdom, 28
    in Vermont, 121–122, 125
    confidence in social institutions, 41–42,
        64, 104

conflict theory, 36–37
Constandriopoulos, A. P., 29n, 30
Cornfield, Daniel, 102n
corporatization, 69, 71, 98
cottage industry, 6, 96–97, 105, 143
Coyne, Patricia, 20, 21
Cunningham, Robert, 19

Daniels, Norman, 16
Davis, James, 42n
Davis, Karen, 43
Davis-Blake, Alison, 102n
de Grandpre, Lili, 90
DeMaria, Alfred, 42
deprofessionalization, 64, 67, 70–71, 99,
   124
Derber, Charles, 98
DeSantis, Grace Budrys, 38
deskilling, 98–100, 104, 108n
Devers, Kelly, 2
"doctor substitute" legislation, 82–84
Doctors' Council, 16–17, 119
Dohler, Marian, 29
Douglas, Joel, 149
Dworkin, James, 95

Eberts, Randall, 146
Edwards, Richard, 96n, 101, 102n, 104,
   148
Ehrenreich, Barbara, 44
Eisenberg, John, 39
Ellis, Norman, 28
Ellwood, Paul, 46, 63, 72
employee status:
   of doctors, 74, 119, 122, 154
   legal definition of, 113
   of residents and interns, 123
Engel, Gloria, 98n, 124
English, Deirdre, 44
Epstein, Arnold, 68
Erikson, Kai, 110
Estill, Jerry, 23
Evans, Robert, 71

Fashoyin, Omotayo, 95
Fein, Rashi, 70

Feldstein, Martin, 60
Fennel, Mary, 98n
Ferber, Stanly, 13, 16
Fligstein, Neil, 109
Form, William, 100n
Freeman, Richard, 102n
free-ridership and UAPD, 127–128
Friedson, Eliot, 36–37, 43–44, 98
functionalism, 34–36

Gallo, Frank, 150
Gamble, Stephen, 19–20
Garfinkel, Simson, 127
Garson, Barbara, 107
Geisen, Gerald, 33
Gettleman, Marvin, 151
Gillies, Rovin, 2
Ginzberg, Eli, 60, 70
Godt, Paul, 25, 29
Golden Age of Medicine, 38–39, 141, 153
Goode, William, 143
Gordon, David, 102n
Gotbaum, Victor, 3
Gouldner, Alvin, 109
Gray, Bradford, 38, 40, 67, 70
Greco, Peter, 39
Greenberg, Warren, 60
grievance procedures and UAPD, 51, 74,
   81, 130–131, 140
Gurman, Richard, 42

Haber, Samuel, 33
Hafferty, Fredric, 33n, 34, 70
Halberstam, Michael, 15, 31
Hall, Richard, 34n, 98n
Halmos, Paul, 37
Hargrove, Barbara, 109
Harrington, Michael, 109
Harrison, Michael, 27
Harrison, Stephen, 28
Hattam, Victoria, 103
Haug, Marie, 70
health sector competition, 59–63
Hechscher, Charles, 101, 103, 143
Heidenheimer, Arnold, 26

Hepner, James, 113
Hirsch, Barry, 96
Hirschman, Albert, 144
Holoweiko, Mark, 76, 87
Hopkins, George, 147
Horty, John, 113
Hsiao, William 54n, 123
Hughes, Everett, 36

iatrogenisis, 44
Iglehart, John, 24–25
Illich, Ivan, 44
Illinois Physicians Union, 12, 56–58, 117,
    122
independent contractor status, 90,
    115–118
individualism, 30–31, 153
industrialization, 6, 96, 99–103, 106
Irwin, Charles, 19
isomorphism, 138
Ito, Hirobumi, 26

Jackson, Pamela, 96n
Jacoby, Sanford, 101
Jellinek, Michael, 97n
Jensen, Joyce, 92n
job actions, 5, 11, 21. See also strikes
Johansen, Lars, 26
Johnson, Dirk, 63, 72
Johnson, Kirk, 92
Johnsson, Julia, 91, 93

Kantor, Rosabeth Moss, 110–111
Kerchner, Charles, 146–147
Kessler-Harris, Alice, 103
Kimball, Bruce, 33
Kirn, Timothy, 3
Klingsberg, Bendix, 26
Klover, Jon, 95
Kochan, Thomas, 96
Kraft, Philip, 110

Larkin, Howard, 2, 39, 97
Larson, Magli Sarfatti, 30, 71
Lefton, Doug, 23
Leicht, Kevin, 98n

Levine, Sol, 38–39, 70–71
Levitan, Sar, 150
Levy, Judith, 33n
Leyerle, Betty, 67, 73n
Liebfried, Stephen, 25
Liebowitz, Barry, 17
Light, Donald, 24, 38–39, 70–71
Linder, Marc, 103n
Lipset, Seymour Martin, 4, 104
Lomas, J., 29n, 30
Luchsinger, Vincent, 95
Luft, Harold, 62

Mallet, Serge, 109–111
malpractice:
    crisis years, 52–56
    rate increase, 19
managed care, 4, 46, 72
managed competition, 125
Mangan, Doreen, 134, 142
Marcus, Sanford:
    and AFL-CIO, 48–49
    and AMA, 87–89
    on benefits to members of UAPD,
        128–130
    on corporate takeover, 97
    on doctors' income, 53–54
    on employee status of doctors, 74,
        113–114
    and organization building, 8–10, 48–56,
        138–140
    and professionalism, 32, 40, 65
    and public attitudes about doctors, 64,
        73
    and right to bargain collectively, 117
Maressa, Vincent, 116
Marmor, Theodore, 97n
Martinelli, Alberto, 100n
McCormick, Brian, 23–24, 91–93, 124–
    125, 142
McCraken, Richard, 119, 121
McDonaldization, 107
McKinlay, John, 33n, 34n, 37, 68n, 70–71,
    98–99
McPherson, David, 96

Meany, George, 48–49
Medi-Cal, 79–82, 89, 135
medical establishment, 43–44, 124–126, 138
Medicare and Medicaid, 29, 43–46, 59, 85, 141
  physicians' reactions to, 12, 76, 129
Medoff, James, 102n
Meyer, Harris, 4, 23, 25, 63, 90, 122, 124, 142
Meyer, John, 68
Michelsen, Ruth, 116
Mitchell, Douglas, 146–147
Mitka, Mike, 2

National Labor Relations Act, 114–115, 120–121
National Labor Relations Board, 21, 114–115, 119–120, 123
Navarro, Vincente, 34n, 98
Nevada Physicians Union, 11–12
new class of workers, 109–111, 154
Norris–La Guardia legislation, 114
Nurcombe, Barry, 97n
nurses, 83–84, 149
  NLRB v. Health Care and Retirement Corporation of America, 120–121

Oberman, Linda, 87, 116
occupational community, 143, 154
organized medicine. See American Medical Association; medical establishment
Owens, Arthur, 61n

Page, Leigh, 124
Pantell, Robert, 19
Parsons, Talcott, 34–35
peer review, 77
Perrow, Charles, 34n, 101
Pfeffer, Jeffrey, 102n
physicians. See also collective bargaining by doctors; strikes
  attitudes on unionism, 11, 15–16, 92
  autonomy of, 13, 36, 72, 98

changing role and professionalism, 35–36, 39–44
employee status of, 74, 119, 122, 123, 154
reasons for joining unions, 12–15, 56–58, 95–96
salaried physicians in UAPD, 4, 52, 128, 130–133, 140
UAPD physicians in private practice, 4, 50, 128, 133–137, 140
Pickney, Deborah, 2
Piore, Michael, 101, 112
Podgursky, Michael, 104
postindustrialism, 106, 109, 112
professional associations, 86–93
professionalism:
  changing definition of, 5–6, 31–33, 37–38
  decline of, 69–72
  dysfunctional aspects of, 36–37
  functions of, 34–36
  inconsistency with unionism, 17, 72, 125, 139
  and large organizations, 98, 141–142
  and new class of workers, 111–112
  in other societies, 30
  as social control mechanism, 66–69
professors and unionism, 149–152. See also Yeshiva University decision
proletarianization, 71, 98–99

Rankin, Tom, 100n
Rayack, Elton, 36
Reich, Robert, 102n, 107–108
Relman, Arnold, 61, 124–125
Resource Based Relative Value Scale (RBRVS), 54n, 60, 123
Richardson, William, 88
Richmond, Julius, 70
Ritzer, George, 34n, 37, 67n, 107
Robinson, Gary, 18–19, 50, 55–56, 128, 131, 133–37
Robinson, James, 2
Roemer, Milton, 24, 66, 99
Rosman, Joseph, 119

Rowland, Diane, 43
Rubin, Beth, 102n
Rueschemeyer, Dietrich, 35
Ruzek, Sheryl, 44

Sabel, Charles, 101
Saltman, Richard, 26
Sammons, James, 72, 91
Scheier, Ronni, 63
Schleslinger, Mark, 97n
Schuller, Alexander, 24
Schwartz, William, 68
Sherman Antitrust Act, 114
Shortell, Stephen, 2
Shostak, Arthur, 17, 146–150
Shryrock, Richard, 36
sickness funds in Germany, 24–25
Skocik, David, 147–148
Sloan, Frank, 62
Smelser, Neil, 100n
Smith, Tom, 42n
Smith, Vicki, 143
Smithey, Richard, 97n
Sobal, Larry, 113
Sommerville, Janice, 3
Spek, Jan-Erik, 29
Starr, Paul, 40–41, 69–70, 98
Steele, Mark, 91
Stelling, Joan, 98n
Stephens, David, 95
Stevens, Rosemary, 43
Stoeckle, John, 71, 98
Stone, Deborah, 24–25
Stone, Joe, 146
Strand, David, 116

strikes, 5, 18, 153, 158
  by British physicians, 28
  by California physicians, 19–20
  by Canadian physicians, 23–24
  by German physicians, 24–25
  by Group Health Association physicians, 20–21
  by Israeli physicians, 27–28
  by teachers in New York City, 146
  unethical, 16

Tarnowieski, Dale, 42
teachers, 65, 145–147
Tennstedt, Florian, 25
Tourain, Alain, 109
Trubo, Richard, 119, 142
Twin Cities, 62–63

Ulrich, Sylvia, 89

Valvona, Joseph, 62

Wagner Act. See National Labor Relations Act
Weinmann, Robert, 1, 127, 133–135
Walczak, David, 34n, 37, 67n
Weisman, Ellen, 27
White, Harrison, 101
Willis, Evan, 28
Witkowski, Kristine, 98n
Wolfe, Samuel, 16, 22
Women's movement, 44
Wolinsky, Frederic, 70

Yeshiva University decision, 119–120, 151